The Stepparent Challenge

STEPHEN J. WILLIAMS, Sc.D.

The Stepparent Challenge

Making It Work

MASTERMEDIA LIMITED • NEW YORK

To the American family,
in its struggle for survival.

Copyright 1993 Stephen J. Williams

All rights reserved, including the right of reproduction in whole or in part in any form. Published by MasterMedia Limited.

MASTERMEDIA and colophon are registered trademarks of MasterMedia Limited.

Library of Congress Cataloging-in-Publication Data
Williams, Stephen J.
 The stepparent challenge : a primer for making it work / Stephen J. Wiliams
   p. cm.
 Includes bibliographical references.
 ISBN 0-942361-72-5 : $13.95
   1. Stepparents—United States.   2. Stepfamilies—United States.
 3. Stepchildren—United States.   4. Remarriage—United States..
 I. Title.
 HQ759.92.W55 1993
 306.8'74–dc20   93–19527
                                                                 CIP

Designed by Jacqueline Schuman
Production Services by Martin Cook Associates, Ltd.
Manufactured in the United States of America.
10 9 8 7 6 5 4 3 2 1

CONTENTS

Preface vii
Introduction ix

Part I: The Challenge 1

1. The Remarriage Dilemma 3
   The Warning 3
   The Basic Dilemma 5
   A Matter of Perspective 7

2. The Changed American Family 9
   The Scary Truth 10
   The Decline of the Nuclear Family 11
   Why We Need to be Concerned 12
   What Does It All Mean? 14

Part II: The Practical Concerns 19

3. The Financial Challenges 21
   Talk It Out 21
   The Cost of Rearing Children 23
   The Early Costs 24
   Growing Up Expensive 26
   Teenagers: Born to Spend 28
   The Biggest Bill of All 34
   Your Estate and Its Disposition 35

4. Rearing Someone Else's Children 41
   Psychological Warfare 43
   New Marriage, New Children 44
   Your Changed Priorities 47
   You Want It Your Way 52
   The Rewards 56

5. Beyond the Challenge: More Complexity 59
   Mixing Religions 60
   Differences of Race and Ethnicity 64
   Differences in Lifestyle Preferences 67
   A Few Other Discreet Issues 67

Part III: The Other People 71

6. Can the New Marriage and Family Survive? 73
   The New Spouse Is Important 74
   The Emotional Effort 75
   The In-laws 77
   The Bottom Line 78

7. The Ex-Spouse 79
   Who Is Responsible? 80
   Who Comes First? 80
   How to Deal with the Ex-spouse 82
   Away We Go 86
   When to Worry 88
   Always Be Ready 90

Part IV: The Commitments and the Answers 93

8. The Ongoing Challenge 95
   So Far Yet So Near 96
   Older Doesn't Mean Better 100
   Life's Uncertainties 102

9. Where Do We Go From Here? 105
   A Look at Your Options 107
   If You Go Ahead 109
   Contemplating Marriage 114
   When It Doesn't Work 116
   And When It Works 117
   Key Points for Success 119

Additional Sources of Information 121
About the Author 125

PREFACE

This book does not provide legal advice, but it does identify situations where such guidance is useful. I advise readers to consult their own attorneys and accountants for further assistance.

The case histories in this book illustrate actual family scenarios. However, the names of individuals have been changed to protect personal privacy.

Since this is a book designed to help people, I wish to thank the many people who helped me by sharing their personal and professional experiences. Their openness and observations were an essential part of this project and I appreciate their generosity.

To Bonnie Kaufman, whose dedication, editorial expertise, and creative talents kept my vision true and on track and to S. Drusilla Jepperson for her assistance in preparing the original manuscript.

And finally, a heartfelt thanks to my publisher, Susan Stautberg, for recognizing the need for this book and for her support in bringing it to print.

INTRODUCTION

What is a family? During the 1992 presidential campaign, the question—thanks in part to a media battle between Vice President Dan Quayle and television's fictitious Murphy Brown—challenged our collective consciousness as never before. Were single parents and their children considered "legitimate" families? Did gay people committed to each other and living together constitute "real" families?

All the permutations and variations of what makes up a family were debated in print, over the airwaves, at the Democratic and Republican national conventions, and at cocktail parties and kitchen tables from coast to coast.

The conclusion? None, really—at least none that could satisfy everyone. And in the end, it was the *question* itself that turned out to be most valuable. It forced us to come to grips with the fact that within one generation, the whole notion of "family" had changed radically—whether we liked it or not. And whether we liked it or not, we as a society needed to deal with these changes, needed to face the truth: that there is no longer one type of family.

Throughout all the public squabbles and political hype, I couldn't dismiss my role as a public health professional and researcher; I am constantly exploring how the social, health, and emotional fabric of our nation can be strengthened. Nor could I dismiss my role as a stepfather.

INTRODUCTION

When I married nearly fifteen years ago, I gladly took on the task of helping to raise two boys who had no biological relationship to me. Looking back now, I had no idea what I was getting myself into; honestly, I hadn't even given it a thought.

Throughout the years, I've encountered problems—as well as joys—that I never anticipated. Issues regarding finances, authority status, marital stress, and more began cropping up. They were simply part of the hidden package of instant parenthood. Clearly, it didn't take long for me to see that one type of family—recently and historically—had been overlooked: The stepfamily.

Still, as the number of stepfamilies has skyrocketed along with the increase in divorce rates, this "new" breed of kinship has taken on various euphemistic incarnations. Briefly, in the mid-1980s, the term "reconstituted family" came into vogue. When that fell out of fashion, along came the "blended family." At the moment, the notion of "blended families" is, more or less, socially acceptable. It is also, according to clinicians who work with these families, unrealistic and philosophically wrong. Families, they argue, *cannot* and *should not* be "blended." Instead, their individual histories must be respected and preserved as the foundation for new lives. Or, as one clinician put it, "Once you try to blend a family, someone is bound to get creamed." So, for the purposes of this book, I have chosen the old, familiar term, "stepfamily".

Through my research, and especially through my own experience, I realized that living with and raising someone else's children is one of the least understood and most challenging roles an adult can take on.

While these family arrangements can work out well, they

often do not. And even when people manage to cope, untangling the complex ties that can bind these families together, as well as strangle them, is rarely easy. In any event, they need to be openly discussed.

This book is written out of a strong belief that nothing ever turns out to be what you expect and that ignorance isn't always bliss.

A Tough Book for a Tough Topic

By nature, Americans are optimistic. We believe that good wins over evil and view life through rose-colored glasses. We seek to overcome adversity and, in large measure, to make the world a better place. But in striving toward these goals, we cannot forgo reality.

With this in mind, I wanted to take a hard-hitting look at stepfamilies without sacrificing reality or optimism. I don't intend to rain on anyone's parade, nor do I gloss over facts. Instead, by realistically examining the challenges of stepfamily life, this book aims to help you understand and prepare for the many crosscurrents of remarriage with children. This goes for stepparents-to-be as well as for those already initiated. I discuss ways of coping with the unique psychological and emotional needs of such families as well as the practical sides of things, such as financial and everyday living arrangements. Above all, I strive to have an honest and insightful discussion and to suggest ways to make it work.

Sometimes It Works

Of course, not *all* remarriages with children are ridden with problems. Sometimes things work out extremely well. And it is certainly important not to create problems that don't exist.

Still, many issues often lie just below the surface, simmering for many years, because neither spouse is willing or able to speak frankly and openly.

With this in mind, it is essential to understand—the sooner, the better—what can happen when everything *looks* rosy. While this book focuses on anticipating and alleviating potential problems, it also can help ensure that problems don't go unrecognized.

Facing the Challenge

This book is divided into four sections. Part I sets the stage and outlines the ramifications of divorce. Part II discusses the practical aspects of remarriage with children: the financial, social, psychological, and emotional issues involved in being a stepparent. It also explores a number of especially difficult situations that can further complicate stepfamily life.

Part III focuses on the other people involved in, or affected by, these marriages, including any children born to the new couple and the many, often trying circumstances that sometimes come with the former spouse.

Part IV provides answers and insights for coping and benefiting from the remarriage, as well as specific suggestions for preparing for such marriages.

Case histories appear throughout the book, illustrating the many scenarios in which people find themselves and how different families have coped. Pointers for coping are also listed throughout, summarizing suggestions from the text.

If you don't already know it, reading this book will drive home the fact that being a stepparent—just as being a natural parent—is far from easy. But keep in mind something that you already *do* know: Nothing in life worth having ever comes easy.

Part One

The Challenge

1

The Remarriage Dilemma

"No one ever told me it was going to be this way!" stepparents often lament. Indeed, even the most psychologically sophisticated people enter stepfamily life with unrealistic assumptions. Few fully anticipate and comprehend the twists and turns they are about to face when they say "I do" to someone who already did and has children to show for it.

All these "instant" parents have to go on are myths and stereotypes. Fairy tales such as Cinderella and Snow White have helped to create the myth of the "wicked stepmother." The stepfather-as-savior stereotype, on the other hand, probably comes from our society's tradition of sexism. In any case, buying into these fantasies is a sure way to do yourself, your marriage, and your stepchildren harm. You are already entering into a tricky situation; the last thing you need are misguided preconceptions.

THE WARNING

Try not to get caught in confusion. Remarriage with children can be a wonderful opportunity to offer a solid family environment for everyone involved. At the same time, however, it can be a source of phenomenal conflict and stress. Understanding the full range of possibilities and how they may affect everyone's life is crucial to coping. Think carefully before you act.

Who's Who?

For the purposes of this discussion, let's be clear about the parties involved and what we will call them. Stepfamilies result from uniting two people, one or both of whom have children from a previous marriage.

Also, there may be more than one prior marriage. The former spouse is the other natural parent of the children being brought up in the new marriage. Again, there may be more than one former spouse. Just think of Johnny Carson or Elizabeth Taylor. Dealing with multiple marriages and different former spouses can get messy, but the basic issues remain the same.

The stepparent is the new spouse. If both spouses have children from previous marriages, then each is a stepparent to the other spouses' children.

The new children are those born into the remarriage; both of the new spouses are their natural parents. Actually, while these definitions help clear the air, it's not really that complicated to figure out the intricacies of these family breaks and ties. Then again, there are some people who have so many husbands or wives and children by different people that it could get quite interesting!

> *The Challenge:* Home, But Hardly Alone
> *Making it Work:* Understanding Responsibility

THE BASIC DILEMMA

Commitment. Over the past several years, the word alone has taken on a popularity that now reaches almost epidemic proportions. When it comes to relationships, and especially to marriage, nearly any form of undesirable behavior is automatically diagnosed as a symptom of "fear of commitment." But what does commitment to a marriage truly mean?

Perhaps Simone Signoret said it best: "Pains do not hold a marriage together. It is the threads, hundreds of tiny threads which sew people together through the years. That's what makes a marriage last—more than passion or even sex."

But marrying with tiny threads already in tow—children—makes for a different kind of wedding knot—and a knot that can be complicated if not downright divisive. That is, a natural parent's loyalties tend to get split between the children and the new spouse—with the new spouse often getting short shrift. The important thing is to remember your wedding vows—even before you make them. The couple must commit to each other absolutely and above all else.

Nonetheless, a kind of tug-of-war goes on. Numerous financial, emotional, psychological, and social stresses grow out of the conflicts between the children's needs and the stepparent's needs.

For instance, say that after allowing for your family's basic expenses and savings, you and your spouse have a little "mad money" leftover. You can spend it any way you want. Sounds simple, right? Sounds like fun? Think again. Imagine that you would like to use it for a weekend getaway with your husband or wife. Your stepchildren, on the other hand, want the newest stereo system on the market—the one that all the other kids in school have. Who decides? However it turns out, chances are that someone is bound to end up being the "bad guy."

Of course, this is just an innocuous scenario. But when medical, dental, and other basic needs enter the equation, the question of who comes first can be a heart-wrenching dilemma for everyone. Further, children born into the new marriage tend to escalate the problem of how financial, emotional, and social resources are allocated. And let's not forget about the former spouse; having to deal with someone's "ex" complicates everything—and often in unpleasant ways.

Make no mistake: these matters must be addressed by *both* partners, preferably before the wedding. If it's too late for that, they can still be dealt with further along. In any case, they're sure to crop up. Gone ignored, they can snowball.

Not only will the couple benefit from frank and open talks, but so too will the stepchildren, as well as any new children. Even for couples remarrying at more advanced ages, these discussions can reduce conflict all around and help lay key issues to rest, such as the disposition of estates.

The Challenge: Conflicting Loyalties and Priorities
Making It Work: Communication, Communication, and more Communication

After reading this book, you may even want to think twice about marrying someone with children. At the least, your eyes will be opened to the particulars of a different, possibly difficult, future. And as romantic as it sounds, the notion of love conquering all may sound profoundly Pollyannaish.

A MATTER OF PERSPECTIVE

Both spouses must understand themselves and each other's perspectives and needs. While the children biologically "belong" to one of the spouses, after remarriage, both the natural parent and the stepparent are responsible for them. Consciously or subconsciously, the stepparent may or may not welcome this.

The natural parent is faced with a juggling act: trying to reconcile the needs of the children with the needs of the spouse, and ultimately, with the needs of the marriage itself. Don't expect miracles; there are no magic solutions. In the worst cases, irreconcilable differences may lead to another divorce. Even so, people can surprise one another. In the best of situations, the new family will provide a stable and happy environment for the stepchildren to grow up in and for the marriage to blossom.

Great National Interest

Over the past twenty years, interest in the changes in family structure has skyrocketed. Scientists have studied and continue to study family trends and their implications for our society and for our children. What's more, psychologists, social workers, and other health care professionals have specialized, expanding their support and counseling services to target stepfamilies.

On the legal and legislative fronts, the courts and state legislatures have had to address the many conflicts that occur in child custody cases and have tried to establish some ground rules. Family law courts, in particular, have struggled with complex, no-win situations. Recent conflicting rulings have, for example, addressed the problem of the custodial spouse's moving far away from his or her ex-spouse and wanting to take the children along. Should the custodial spouse be allowed to do so, recognizing that visitations would be much less frequent, much more difficult, and much more expensive as a result? That's only one of a plethora of questions.

The Setting in Review

Marriage in any form isn't easy. If it were, there wouldn't be so many divorces. Marriage with children is even more challenging, but the opportunities for a better, more fulfilling life for everyone are great. Avoiding the pitfalls and reaping the benefits of stepfamily life should be everyone's goal. And having a little help along the way can't hurt.

It's always nice to know that you're not alone. There are lots of people in this boat. And as rocky as the waters sometimes may seem, no one has to be shipwrecked.

2

The Changed American Family

Grab your television's remote control, flip through the channels, and prepare yourself for a brief history lesson. Nostalgia for the Kennedy era is all the rage now, and sitcoms from the 1950s and '60s are perfuming the airwaves. Take a good sniff. It won't take long to realize that shows such as *Ozzie and Harriet, Leave It to Beaver, Father Knows Best, Dennis the Menace,* and others all portrayed family life as one long holiday during which everyone was euphorious all the time. Sure, Dennis could create a thirty-minute catastrophe by losing his pet gerbil, but in the end, everyone was bound to live happily-ever-after.

Even *The Brady Bunch,* one of the first shows of the 1970s to acknowledge the existence of stepfamilies, failed to acknowledge reality; again, life was a cinch.

Right or wrong, this by-gone cultural vision of the American family was what our society wanted to think of as "normal." Despite what went on in real life, most people aspired to this fantasy, or at the very least, they tried to fake it. Divorce, children born out of wedlock, homosexuality, and frictions in general were taboo. They existed of course, but only in a dark silence.

Now, take a look at today's television families. In one form or another, they all share troubles. Learning disabilities, loneliness, rape, AIDS, death, infertility, and divorce are commonplace; "normal" just isn't what it used to be.

Throughout these incarnations, two things have become clear: our nation can survive—and even benefit—from openness, and its mental and social health doesn't necessarily depend on *how* families are organized. Nonetheless, we need to put these changes in perspective.

THE SCARY TRUTH

Statistics tend to be real eye-openers and the statistics on the American family—and especially on divorce—can be shocking. But before we talk about actual numbers, let's take a look at their relevance.

The effect of divorce on children's mental and physical health is a concern we all must share. And for the future's sake, we need to give children a higher priority than we do adults. Just the same, no one escapes untouched.

If you divorce and you don't have children, both you and your former spouse can go on with your lives with no biological strings attached. But divorce with children is a completely different story—and the ending isn't always a happy one. Profound long-term implications for the former spouse, for the new spouse, and for the children can read like a soap opera.

Naturally, a healthy family environment is essential for healthy child development—especially when the child is young and most impressionable. It only makes sense, then, that the growing numbers of children caught in the web of divorce may be weaving a bad omen. Likewise, children and anyone else trapped in destructive but intact marriages may be candidates for physical abuse, neglect, the effects of drug and alcohol abuse, and many other wounds that leave lasting scars. Indeed, instability robs everyone of a healthy, rich life.

THE DECLINE OF THE NUCLEAR FAMILY

With all this in mind, consider some of the statistics:

- About one-half of all marriages end in divorce.
- Less than half of all American families are traditional nuclear families.
- More than one-fifth of all U.S. households are now headed by single parents.
- More than one-fifth of all children are born to single women.
- Every year, at least one million children are involved in marital break-ups.
- More than 40 percent of our nation's children will see their parents' marriage end before they turn 16.

Startling trends to say the least, trends that say a lot about society. And they don't stop there. In 1965, 10.1 percent of all American families were single-parent families. By 1985—about a generation later—this figure shot up to 22.2 percent. In other words, nearly one out of every four families is currently headed by single parents.

American births are another troubling issue. In 1965, 7.7 percent of all births were to unmarried women. Twenty years later, that number had nearly tripled.

THE CHALLENGE

WHY WE NEED TO BE CONCERNED

The nation's more than 1,000,000 divorces each year involve more than 1,000,000 children. Figure 1 dramatically shows the change in the numbers of divorces and the number of children involved over the last 40 years. Or in plain words, the number has tripled. And this only accounts for children under 18.

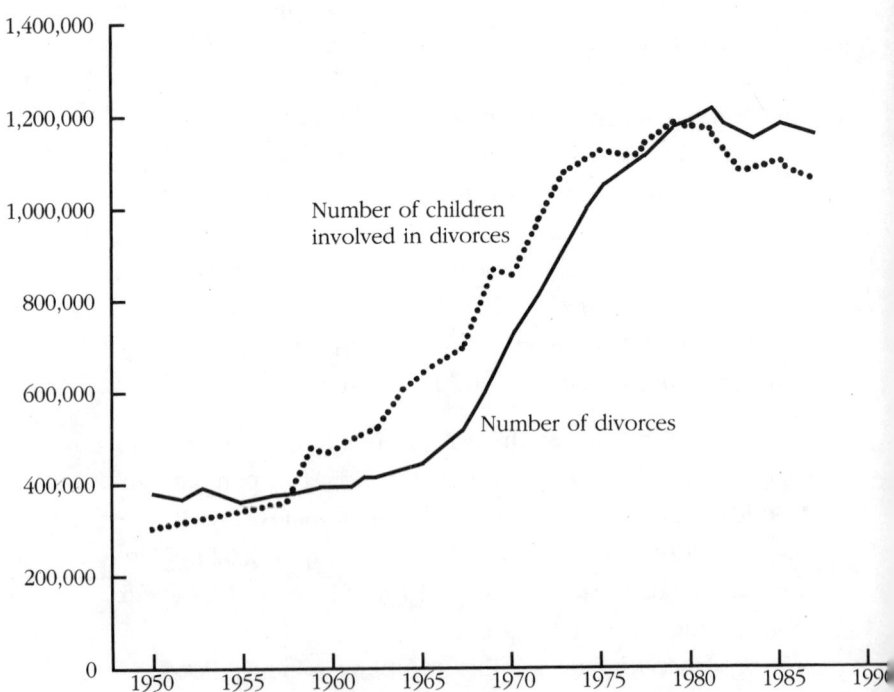

Recently, the number of divorces has leveled off slightly. Thus, the slight decline in the number of children of divorce is simply a result of people's having fewer children and fewer divorces. It doesn't necessarily translate into any great long-term improvement in the situation.

Naturally, the longer people are married, the more likely they are to have children. Therefore, only 12 percent of those who divorce before their first anniversaries have children together. This number jumps to 60 percent for those married between five and nine years, and to 75 percent after 10 to 14 years.

Demographic, psychological, and sociological studies have looked at the impact of children on marriage. They have found that having children can't "save" a troubled marriage. In fact, the opposite is true: the normal stresses that come with children can provoke divorce in inherently weak relationships.

Other studies have looked at how divorce affects children. In most cases, divorce is likely to hurt them and may inhibit their development in a number of ways. Unless a marriage is truly miserable, the old notion of staying together "for the sake of the children" may not be such a ludicrous idea. Either way, however, someone is likely to suffer.

Recent research has come up with these results about the children of divorce:

- Divorce and remarriage are strongly correlated with socioeconomic status. The proportion of children living in low-income families ranges from 11 percent for those living with both biological parents to 66 percent for those living with never-married mothers.
- Although family structure is not associated with most

measures of physical health, children of divorce are more likely to have accidents and injuries.
- Children not living with both biological parents are at greater risk of having behavior and performance problems in school.
- Children living with a mother only, or with a mother and a stepfather, are two to three times more likely to be expelled or suspended from school than are children from traditional families.
- Behavior problems as well as anxiety, depression, hyperactivity, dependency, peer conflict, and social withdrawal are least likely for children living with both biological parents, slightly higher for those living with never-married mothers, and highest for those living with divorced mothers or with mothers and stepfathers.

WHAT DOES IT ALL MEAN?

Despite the divorce rate, our nation's marriage rate has remained relatively stable. Every year, approximately one in one hundred people marry. The most significant statistical blip occurred at the end of World War II; as soldiers returned from battle, "settling down" became the thing to do. People were eager to get on with "normal" life and postwar prosperity and optimism—along with the G.I. Bill's endorsement of cheap mortgages, free tuition, low interest loans to start businesses, and special allowances for G.I. wives and children—all campaigned strongly for family life. Thus, the ever-popular baby-boom generation was born.

It is this generation that has created a new and different demographic landscape. For one thing, babyboomers tend to marry later in life than did their parents. Since 1950, according to the United States Census Bureau, the median age for marrying has jumped up from 22.8 to 26.3 years for men, and from 20.3 to 24.1 years for women. And possibly, the longer one delays marriage, the more likely he or she is to end up in a stepfamily.

Now, let's take a look at remarriage. Of every one hundred women, forty-one of them will remarry. Meanwhile, the remarriage rate for men is slightly higher; forty-five out of one hundred will recite their vows for at least a second time. And, despite their past experiences, divorced people are *more* likely to take the leap than are widowed people as well as those who never married.

MEDIAN REMARRIAGE AGE

	If Previously Divorced	*If Previously Widowed*
Women	32.8	54.6
Men	36.1	62.7

What's more, they don't waste time. About one-third of men and women remarry within a year of their divorces. Half of all divorced and widowed men remarry within about two years. And half of all divorced women remarry in approximately two-and-a-half-years.

Also, the younger people are, the more likely they are to get divorced. Divorce rates for women are highest for those under 20; for men, the highest rate is for those aged 20 to 24.

While older people tend to show greater stability, it's difficult to predict how the babyboomers will handle their senior years. As they head toward retirement, their divorce rates may set new records. In the end, the state of the marital union may come down to the state of the union in general; social and economic issues have a strong influence on divorce trends.

At present, a little more than 70 percent of divorcing men and women are ending their first marriages. Another 21 percent or so are ending their second marriages. The rest have gone around at least three times.

There is some good news, though: as people mature, their marriages have a greater likelihood of surviving. And if one does get divorced and remarried later in life, their new marriage will probably be more stable, too.

STARTING OVER

John London was a 38-year-old attorney. Divorced and childless, he fell in love with Mary Adamson. Mary was 33, college-educated, and also divorced. She had two children: Andrea, 12, and Howard (known as Howie), 10, both from her previous marriage.

As Mary and John were about to wed, both were a little apprehensive. Yet they also looked forward to a happy family life and even considered having children together.

John was reasonably successful, so he wasn't overly concerned about the minimal financial support that Mary had received from her ex-husband. And Mary hoped to keep working as an administrative assistant to a corporate bigwig.

As it turned out, after six years of marriage, the couple seemed to be doing well. Andrea had started college, and Howie was finishing his sophomore year of high school. Also, John and Mary were happy and fortunate to have two children of their own. All in all, the family appeared to be getting along reasonably well.

Still, there was some friction between the older kids. Howie, in particular, was somewhat rebellious and seemed to blame his stepfather for the discord between Mary and her former husband—a man who had refused to provide any college support for either of his children.

Just the same, John and Mary enjoyed the life that they had created together. They felt that they would make it through family tensions and difficult times. They loved raising their own children, and while they were still somewhat apprehensive about the future, they were, nonetheless, optimistic that things would continue to work out reasonably well.

In summary, these numbers tell a complex story. The nature of American marriage has changed dramatically. We live in a different world from previous generations. Our family life faces a new set of realitites. We must adapt and change to accomodate this new world.

Part Two

The Practical Concerns

3

The Financial Challenge

No matter how devastating divorce may feel, life does go on. And when it comes to raising children of divorce, not only do life's financial obligations go on, but they also pose serious matters for both the natural parents and for the stepparent. Along with the other responsibilities of instant parenthood, a stepparent who marries someone of average means may very well expect that at least some of the financial stresses that come with raising children will fall on his or her shoulders.

The Challenge: Who Gets What?
Making It Work: Understanding and Agreement

TALK IT OUT

If you're like most people, economic issues are important to you. And what happens to your future earnings and to your entire estate may be greatly affected by marrying someone with children.

Unfortunately, discussing finances doesn't exactly ignite romance. What's more, most of us are loath to raise what may appear to be self-serving issues. The natural parent may misinterpret money-talk as a rejection of the new family. If this is the case, perhaps your relationship itself isn't terribly strong to begin with. Nonetheless, economic complexities of remarriage, combined with possible financial problems with the former spouse, can make for a touchy and tough scenario.

Mature adults, however, face facts; sooner or later the bill always comes due. Better to figure things out and plan ahead than to have a battle later on over who pays for what.

Children born into the new family raise more questions about the allocation of limited resources; needs of the "first" and the "second" families can turn into competitions. However you choose to address these matters—rationally or irrationally—keep in mind that the bottom line is always the bottom line.

The Challenge: Fair Financing
Making It Work: Options and Agreements

Some Early Options

If you haven't called a caterer yet, call a lawyer. Premarital agreements are useful if one or both spouses-to-be have major assets. The agreement is merely a mechanism for deciding how the marriage will "operate," and not necessarily an expression of cynicism. To carry the most legal weight, these contracts must be drawn up by attorneys, with separate representation for each person.

While premarital agreements are generally considered contrived and unromantic, they are becoming more and more acceptable, especially where stepfamilies are concerned. It's simply a matter of practicality. Even after the wedding, legal agreements can clear the air and help to cope with unforeseen circumstances.

Another approach calls for each spouse to keep his or her assets separate. To understand the implications of separate finances, legal advice is once again valuable, especially where community property estates are concerned. Each spouse can contribute to the joint household expenses, while the spouse (or spouses) with the children is responsible for their bills.

THE COST OF REARING CHILDREN

Stepchildren or natural children, it doesn't matter: raising kids is a costly venture. Generally speaking, child-rearing expenses include:

- Medical and dental costs and insurance
- Food
- Housing
- Education and enrichment
- Travel (including vacations and visitations)
- Entertainment and extra-curricular activities
- Gifts
- Automobile insurance, registration, gasoline, and maintenance

The former spouse may help to offset some of these expenses. As discussed in a later chapter, it's probably foolhardy to count on your husband's or wife's "ex" to help foot the bill for as long as the costs of parenthood continue. Considering the many hidden expenses involved in raising children, custodial parents rarely receive fair financial support from their old "other half."

So regardless of whether you realize it, instant parenthood means instant payments. Like all children, stepchildren can't time their needs to suit your budget or convenience; needs begin whenever—even immediately. For example, say that right during your wedding reception, your brand-new stepdaughter has an appendicitis attack and needs to get to an emergency room pronto. You can't sit around and hash out who is going to cough up the quarter to call for an ambulance, let alone ruminate over upcoming medical expenses.

The Challenge: Life is Expensive, Especially When It's Not Yours
Making It Work: Clearing Up the Questions

The costs of raising children can continue almost endlessly. And as children grow, so do their expenses—somehow far exceeding rises in inflation rates.

THE EARLY COSTS

Before birth, there are bills. To be sure, the costs of bringing children through their formative years are many and varied. And when you are bringing up stepchildren, the equation can get even more complicated. Obviously, how old the children are at the time of a remarriage determines the kinds of expenses, as well as the total lifetime costs, you may incur. A rule of thumb: the younger the children, the greater the bills—and the higher they pile up over the years!

Health Care Costs

For infants, huge medical expenses begin with prenatal and postnatal care. If the baby has any type of congenital illness, the bills can be substantial. A single day in the hospital for a newborn can exceed $3,000, not to mention simple surgical procedures that may add up to thousands more.

The Challenge: Not Letting Health Care Break the Bank
Making It Work: You Can Never Have Too Much Insurance or Too Many Agreements

Fortunately, stepchildren can be covered on health insurance policies—even if you have employer-sponsored insurance. To avoid potential financial ruin, this coverage is imperative. But there's a hitch: many employers require their workers to pay part or all of the premium cost when they add more children to their policies.

To make the most out of your due:

- Coordinate policies between both natural parents and stepparents as a means of lowering costs.
- Add stepchildren to policies immediately after marriage.
- Know the liabilities for children with serious physical, mental, psychological, or social problems.
- Be aware that full-time students can usually be covered only until age 21 to 23.
- Consider managed-care plans (HMO, PPO, and so on) which may offer more comprehensive benefits, less paper work, and easier access.
- Realize that low-income earners should qualify for Medicaid or other assistance programs.

If both spouses are insured through their jobs, it may be possible to provide more comprehensive coverage by coordinating benefits. A former spouse should also be able to cover minors under his or her policy. But if added premium expenses are part of the deal, he or she may not be so eager to comply. A court order or a divorce decree can "encourage" a former spouse to chip in.

Most policies require co-payments and deductibles where you pay part of all expenses. Some costs associated with children's health care needs are not covered at all. For instance, certain plans do not cover well-child care, immunizations, vaccinations, and other basics of preventive medicine. When it comes to routine home care, over-the-counter drugs such as cough syrup and aspirin are rarely covered at all. Also, procedures required to correct pre-existing conditions such as birth defects may not be covered and payment may have to come out of your pocket.

In more complex cases, children with serious ailments often need great financial, as well as emotional, support. Those with chronic disabilities, mental health problems, or severe physiological impairments may require at-home, professional help. At worst, you may end up in a rare yet devastating situation, having to deplete nearly all of your resources to qualify for public assistance.

Of course, health care expenses continue as long as children are minors—and often beyond. Still, other needs remain that may not be met by insurance: dental care, particularly reconstructive and oral surgery, and orthodontia. Dental care is often only partially covered by employers, if they cover it at all. In fact, many people have no dental insurance.

GROWING UP EXPENSIVE

Health care is only the beginning of the costs of raising children. Infants and toddlers need clothes, food, diapers, toys, furniture, and baby paraphernalia *galore*. Again, don't count on the baby's non-custodial parent to share these expenses. And down the line, bills grow. You may need a larger family car for a larger family. The same goes for a house or an apartment, and all the heating and air conditioning bills that are part of that package. And if you have teenagers at home, you can automatically multiply electric and phone bills.

The Challenge: Costs Are Always More than You Expect
Making It Work: Plan for the Unexpected

Who minds the kids when parents aren't around? Unlike yesteryear when grandparents and other family members lived in close proximity and were available to baby-sit for free, today's mobile society has changed all that. Today, many husbands and wives work outside the home and have no built-in support system to count on. That leaves professional child care which can be expensive, easily running from $100 a week and up. This may not include charges for after-hours care, pick-up and delivery of the child, lunch, and other extras.

THE COSTS GROW FASTER THAN THE CHILDREN

As children grow, so do their needs. Take the basics—food, housing, clothing—and add on the "finer things of life." The list may seem nearly endless. Music lessons . . . ballet classes . . . birthday parties . . . holiday gifts. . . .

Who pays? Whoever is willing to foot the bill, that's who. And the stepparent can expect to do his or her share—or more. Even if money is scarce, it may be hard to say no to a child's educational, cultural, social, and entertainment needs.

You'll notice children becoming more aware of the world around them by the way they learn to rack up bills; their expectations become higher and higher and along with that, their sense of materialism tends to grow and grow. Take fashion trends: if $200 sneakers happen to be the latest in kiddie vogue, chances are that your youngsters will want them, even feel that they *need* them. Socializing becomes a more costly endeavor as well.

Indeed, opportunities for spending lots of money are unlimited, as are the bills. Depending on the extent to which the children and the former spouse help out with expenses, the true cost of remarriage with children can add up fast.

TEENAGERS: BORN TO SPEND

The teenage years are when expenditures really blossom. For adolescents, peer pressure mounts and keeping up may become even more urgent; no kid wants the risk of being stigmatized as a nerd. So hanging out with the "right" crowd, participating in the "right" school activities, as well as the "right" cultural pursuits, clubs, sports, and perhaps summer camp can eat up a family budget.

But don't close that wallet yet. You may be faced with even more chances to spend, spend, spend. There's always the possibility of private school, with tuitions that can start at a few thousand dollars a year and keep climbing. And don't forget your stepchild's visits to the other natural parent, who may have moved across the country.

Even so, generalizations are unfair; no two children are alike. Priorities for spending—and saving—varies greatly. Occasionally, youngsters recognize that their parents aren't bottomless automated teller machines, always available for easy and unlimited withdrawls.

Children can even rein in costs themselves, but don't expect them to do so without parental discipline. The more restraint, the less the financial stress on the marriage.

To help yourself and your children:

- Set limits
- Be sure that both natural parents send the same messages
- Ditto for the stepparent and the natural parent
- Encourage children to earn their own money
- Develop and stick to a budget
- Be clear about what you will pay for
- Establish an economic ethic for the family

None of this will work unless parents enforce ground rules—a difficult task. Indeed, many parents don't do a great job of instilling the importance of thrift and saving. And a natural parent who harbors guilt over his or her divorce and its impact on the children may not have the emotional wherewithal to do this. Further, living in a society that makes instant gratification the norm thanks to credit cards, and promotes spending by and for children certainly doesn't help.

But the financial outlook need not be hopeless. Children can help out by working part-time. If overdone, however, this may be detrimental to academic achievement and social activities. On the other hand, besides earning money, many kids learn useful skills and benefit from part-time work. And for those who don't go on to college, part-time work during high school years can be a head start on a career.

Total Shock: Cars

For many parents, the real financial shock hits when the children are old enough to tune into the car's radio, crank the volume up all the way, and not have anyone around telling them to keep their eyes on the road. For kids, taking control of the steering wheel for the first time is a kind of coming-of-age ritual. Just think back to the time when you got your driver's license and you'll be able to appreciate the emotional experience of the moment. It bestows new-found freedom. Suddenly, you can come and go at will without having to rely on someone else and without supervision.

The Challenge: The Risky Road—for the Parents
Making It Work: Insure! Insure! Insure!

Ideally, your stepchildren will have no urge to drive at all. Then again, this probably is a sign that your kids aren't *quite* normal. Be thankful then that they have healthy urges, dig up your auto insurance policy, and read carefully.

For most policy-holders, insurance costs drop significantly if the child qualifies for good-student and driver-training discounts.

Some other insurance considerations include:

- Making sure that the child is on the custodial parent's policy
- Carrying high liability limits
- Obtaining an umbrella liability policy
- Looking for these discounts: multiple car, good driver, low mileage per year, air bag, and car alarm
- Raising deductibles
- Buying an inexpensive car
- Requiring the child to have good grades in order to use the car
- Putting the car and policy in the child's name when he or she is no longer a minor

STICKER SHOCK

George Allen spent his life working hard. As a plumber, he put in long hours and lots of sweat to make a decent, but not luxurious, living. The way he saw it, it was all worth it; his work, he felt, wasn't just benefiting himself alone.

George had married his high-school sweetheart, Beth Eaton. Actually, the two had lost touch for about fifteen years after graduation. During that time, Beth had married, had a daughter, Mary, and divorced. But it was the first time that wedding bells ever rang for George.

When Mary was about to turn 16, her new stepfather taught her how to drive. She had also taken driver's education at school, where she was an excellent student.

George and Beth had already changed their insurance to cover both themselves and their cars. As a result, their total bill turned out to be less than before they got married.

Then Mary passed her road test and got her license. Her stepfather dutifully reported her success to the insurance company.

Unfortunately, he wasn't quite prepared for the surprise that arrived a few days later: a bill for $365—and for only six months' coverage! When he called his agent, he found out that he lived in a high-cost area, that auto insurance was no longer less expensive for girls than for boys, and that Mary had already gotten good-student, multi-car and driver-education discounts.

With some trepidation, George asked what would happen to his insurance costs if Mary got an old "beater" car. Again, he wasn't prepared for the news: the bill would double! The next day, he asked his boss if he could work extra hours on weekends.

THE PRACTICAL CONCERNS

Make sure to study your insurance quote, or the first bill that arrives after your youngster gets his or her driver's license. Keep in mind that these costs vary from family to family, from region to region, and from circumstance to circumstance.

Adding a new driver to your auto insurance may hike up your bill by anywhere from $200 to $2,000 a year. In all likelihood, these expenses will only go up as expenses have a way of doing.

If the whole thing sounds unaffordable, there are other options worth considering. For one, you can simply refuse to let the child have a driver's license. This may be workable in cities with good public transportation—at least for a few years. But aside from potential tension and resentment, you may be left having to chauffeur the youngster everywhere; there is a convenience in having another driver in the family. In this case, the child can contribute to car costs by working part-time.

Usually, the only car-related expense greater than insurance is the actual car. And what teenager doesn't want a car? Of course, that price tag greatly depends on the make, condition, and age of the vehicle.

If you buy an old clinker, you can count on substantial repair bills, especially if the youngster fails to take care of the car. Also, insurance, and especially collision and comprehensive coverage, is subject to numerous variables. A newer car, for instance, costs more initially, and the insurance bills will be higher. And remember to plan for operating costs such as gasoline, inspections, and tune-ups. Further, any repairs resulting from various mishaps, such as replacing your garage door after it has been driven through, have to be taken into account as well.

There are other—and more dangerous—risks. If your youngster is a minor and is at fault for an accident, you may be held liable for damages. Should a *real* tragedy occur and someone is killed or seriously injured, the liability could be enormous.

Your insurance company should cover you up to the maximum limits of your policy and stepchildren are covered the same as natural children. If you are not the custodial parent, be sure your children are covered when they come for a visit.

Most people are under-insured. If major injuries occur in an accident, the costs of health care, repairs, and damages can be in the hundreds of thousands or even millions of dollars. In other words, you could be wiped out. If you're not, these costs could still exceed the limits of your policy and you may be paying off claims for years.

So don't skimp on safety. Even people of modest means should have at least $100,000 worth of coverage. You can get protection by signing up for a relatively inexpensive umbrella policy, an outstanding value for anyone with children.

Generally, insurance is required for all drivers in a household and the custodial parent is usually the one who carries the youngster on his or her policy. Also, depending on what state you live in, it may be a good idea to put title to the car and the insurance in the youngster's name when he or she is no longer a minor. Your insurance agent and lawyer can best advise you in these situations. Remember: the likelihood of a tragedy is low, but even highly responsible people have accidents.

THE BIGGEST BILL OF ALL

College: even preparing to apply can really test your budget. First there are the fees to take the SATs, and if necessary, expensive review courses for the test. Next are the actual school application fees. And who wants to trust the next four years of their lives to a place they've only seen in slick brochure photographs? Visits to campuses alone—including transportation fees, hotel stays, taxis, meals—are costly, hidden ventures.

The Challenge: Paying for College
Making It Work: Plan Ahead and Don't Leave the Ex-Spouse Out

Consider the variables: your child can go to a private school or a public school, live at home or away, qualify for financial aid or not, and so on. All in all, it's best to prepare for astronomical bills.

In some states, parents may not be legally required to pay for college. But would you want to be the one to deny a college education to a motivated student?

College usually lasts for four years, but some students need more time than that. If your youngster decides to get an advanced degree—or degrees—you could be looking at another one to five years of education-related expenses.

Many financial aid programs are available, although these are becoming more difficult to qualify for; contributions expected from students and their parents, including stepparents, are escalating. Certain financial aid programs expect contributions from the ex-spouse—contributions that may never materialize.

Again, students can offset expenses by working or participating in work-study programs. But depending on the person, there may be a trade-off in terms of academic performance. And of course, if the stepparent and the natural parent each have children of their own, they will face increased costs from both sides.

Another way to save on expenses is to have the student live at home and attend a nearby public college. But take into account the seemingly small expenses that can add up to a hefty price tag: books, supplies, socializing, transportation, and other necessities; even a "bare bones" budget may need some filling out. And keep in mind that living with an adult other than your spouse may be highly stressful and depending on the maturity and personality of the young adult—as well as the older adults—the arrangement may not be worth it.

At the other extreme, packing the youngster off to a high-quality—or at least high-cost—private school could easily come to between $15,000 and $30,000 a year, considering tuition and fees, room and board, transportation, long-distance telephone calls, and all the rest. And note: these figures are expressed in *today's* dollars, without regard to tomorrow's inflation rates.

YOUR ESTATE AND ITS DISPOSITION

It's not uncommon for people to overlook or fail to understand the long-range financial implications of marrying someone with children, or remarrying when they have children of their own. And the implications are many. Remarriage with children can have tremendous, and often unintended effects on the disposition of your estate. What happens to family heirlooms when you have natural children and stepchildren?

THE PRACTICAL CONCERNS

Do you smash a prized vase into pieces so that everyone gets a share? Who gets what pieces? What's fair?

To be sure, fairness is more subjective than many of us realize. You could, for example, have stepchildren who are more devoted to you than your natural children are. Does that make them more deserving? Or does that fact that they aren't biologically related to you make them less deserving? Is everyone equal? What kind of impact will your decisions regarding your estate have on those you leave behind? All kinds of feelings—love, hate, jealousy, power, guilt, and so on—are attached to money. Moreover, no one likes to think about death.

Obviously then, the entire issue of writing a will is a highly emotional and complex one—an issue that many parents, as well as children, have great difficulty facing. For that very reason, it's in everyone's best interest for you to deal with the matter thoughtfully, carefully, and intelligently.

The Challenge: Making Sure that Your Wishes Are Carried Out
Making It Work: See a Lawyer Immediately

In many states, assets accumulated during a marriage and not held separately may automatically go to your spouse when you die. While this is especially important for those marrying later in life, it concerns everyone who marries. If your spouse has children, particularly minors, your assets may end up in their hands, rather than going to your natural children. This is certainly fine if that's what you want—but you must be clear about what you want.

In any case, get legal counsel so that your wishes are carried out to the letter. Otherwise, if you die without leaving a will or a trust, your assets will be distributed according to the laws of the state regardless of your desires.

For example, your spouse brings two children into the marriage from a previous marriage. Then you have two children together. Without proper legal preparation, and again depending on your state's laws, it's possible that upon your death your estate will go entirely to your spouse. Then, upon his or her death, these assets may be distributed among your stepchildren as well as the children you had together.

You may have wanted to leave your assets exclusively to your biological children. But don't count on it unless you've made advance preparations. Even worse, after your death, your widow or widower might remarry, taking all your former assets into his or her new marriage. If that happens, your estate could be spread among even more people and may eventually end up in the hands of his or her new spouse.

THE ASSETS THAT GOT AWAY

Robert Lotten died, leaving two children, Steven and Brenda. He was a great father, totally devoted to his kids. And since their mother had died eight years earlier, Steven and Brenda had no blood relatives left.

About seven years earlier, though, Robert had remarried. His new wife, Linda Carter, had two children of her own, Mike and Todd. But Steven and Brenda never really got along with them—or with Linda, for that matter.

After the funeral, Linda told Steven and Brenda that their father had signed a simple will that he and Linda had written themselves. The will left everything to her.

Robert was a very successful businessman whose estate was

quite substantial. He had never hesitated to consult lawyers for his business matters, but he seemed to have an aversion to do the same where is personal life was concerned. Well aware of this, Steven and Brenda had urged him to hire an attorney and write a premarital agreement. He refused.

Now what were they to do? Since it was hardly likely that their stepmother would give them a penny, they consulted an attorney on their own. But during probate, their father's will was declared valid. Steven and Brenda felt that they had lost out and that their father's true desires—had he planned better—would have included them.

Most people have far more assets than they realize; often they simply overlook the value of their worldly possessions. Just take a casual look around your home. Furniture, china, appliances, jewelry, artwork, and all the rest have worth, be it monetary or sentimental. When children from different marriages are involved, and each spouse has his or her own assets—plus jointly accumulated assets—deciding where everything will wind up can add up to a thorny equation. And even if you have very few possessions, it may mean a lot to you to know that they will go to the people of *your*—and not your state's—choice.

No doubt, the degree to which you want to provide for your spouse's children from previous marriages, if at all, should be your decision. The protection of your own children and other family members is your duty and obligation. And, of course, this is not a situation that can be easily dealt with after the fact.

So *before* the fact you may consider:

- Knowing the value of your assets before you marry and deciding where you want them to go when you die
- Consulting an attorney who is experienced in estate trusts
- Setting up a trust
- Writing a will
- Discussing estate issues with your spouse
- Deciding who should be the administrator and the executor of your estate

A Few Other Details

Family businesses and other complex situations require even more legal planning to assure that assets end up where you want them to. Thinking and acting ahead can also reduce taxes and administrative costs. By the same means, personal belongings and other untitled assets can also be passed along according to one's wishes.

Also, pay special attention to the way you handle property, especially real estate. How your holdings are titled is extremely important. Recording ownership as tenants-in-common, and using a trust, is essential if you want to leave such assets to your own children only. Passing everything to your spouse may mean that some property rights will not end up where you had intended them to.

A qualified terminable interest property (QTIP) election to a trust or a will can direct remaining assets to one's own children. Combined with a living trust, assets can assist the natural parent when you die. This way, the principal goes to the stepparent's biological children when he or she dies. There may also be tax advantages associated with these arrangements.

During the enthusiasm of romance, or even during the

realities of everyday married life, none of this is easy to accomplish. The financial side of being a stepparent is only one, and in some respects not even the most important, aspect of your challenge. But if you and your spouse do not address this issue of remarriage with children, they may be dealt with for you by others.

4

Rearing Someone Else's Children

The first relationship that we have in our lives is our relationship with our parents. For that very reason, it's a highly emotional and powerful one, one that influences the shape of our personalities and the course of our lives.

So what happens when you disrupt that most basic of all bonds and then add a stepparent? What can you, as a stepparent, expect and what will be expected of you? It's almost impossible to know, given all the variables involved. Are you entering the marriage as a seasoned parent with children of your own or are you a novice? How old are your stepchildren? What's their background? What kind of relationship do they have with their natural parents? How long has it been since their parents divorced? What's your new spouse like? The questions are virtually endless.

The only thing you can be sure of is that you are entering an emotionally and socially complicated situation—and not a fairy tale existence in which everyone is happy because remarriage is somehow mistaken as a means of instant family "repair." Remarriage doesn't repair anything. The formation and dynamics of stepfamily life are trying on everyone and you can't be a "successful" stepparent without some notion of what you are getting yourself into, or without the natural parent's understanding and support.

The Challenge: The Stepfamily Is Not a Natural Biological Match

Making It Work: Understand the Dynamics in Advance; Accept Reality; Work at It

The psychological undercurrents involved in remarriage are fantastically complex. Freud wrote volumes on the importance of the child-parent relationship—and that was well before divorce reached epidemic proportions. So none of us should be surprised when divorce raises havoc in a child's social and emotional development. But we still have to cope with the after-effects.

For a child, remarriage symbolizes the permanent "dumping" of the other natural parent. It closes off the possibility that the natural parents will ever reunite—a wish that many children of divorce have. The whole situation may create terrific tension in a child's mind. Think about what divorce—and remarriage—must be like from a young child's perspective. Even grown children harbor these feelings.

There are no hard and fast rules or commonly accepted notions about relationships in stepfamilies. The nature and realities of blended families vary from marriage to marriage. Sometimes children from a prior marriage are a welcome bonus. But in many—and probably most—marriages, these children represent a trying addition to the family.

PSYCHOLOGICAL WARFARE

The most difficult aspect of being a stepparent is that stepchildren usually retain their allegiance to the natural parents. Even if the former spouse is estranged from the children, their underlying loyalty and devotion, however expressed, will likely hold fast. That's life.

These feelings may be suppressed in the face of the child's day-to-day life. But they can surface at any time and in many ways. That, in part, can cause strain in the stepchild's relationship with the new parent. Some warning signs that children are having difficulties are:

- Hostility toward the stepparent before marriage
- Behavioral problems and social-adjustment difficulties
- School problems
- Few friends
- Unusual introversion
- Refusal to take direction from, or interact with, the future stepparent
- Physical violence
- Destructive behavior

The quality of the relationship between children and the stepparent also depends on several other factors: how old the children are when the divorce and remarriage occurs, whether the former spouse is alive or dead, and how well the natural parents get along after divorce. Another thing to consider is that any social or emotional problems that children may have before divorce are likely to worsen after divorce.

Still, the new marriage may help stabilize the child's life. This is more likely if the child has come out of an abusive marriage or if the former spouse is dead.

These tensions and crosscurrents can play themselves out in the child's relationship with the stepparent. There may be a high degree of animosity. The child may play one parent against another. "Acting out" and other behavioral patterns can reflect the child's underlying feelings regarding the natural parents and the divorce. And you'd better believe that none of this makes for a picnic. As a stepparent, you may have to live with constant hostility.

Many of the emotions and relationship issues are similar for stepmothers and stepfathers. Much depends on the personalities involved. How strong is the stepparent? Who wields the power in the family?

A stepparent who shares custodial responsibility for the children faces these matters every day. Even when the new spouse is not the custodian, the child may use visits as an opportunity to make clear his or her feelings against the stepparent. Some children never outgrow their desire to see the new marriage end.

As any parent knows, children can make life both miserable and rewarding. But this balance is totally thrown off when *someone else's child* makes your life miserable with temper tantrums, antagonistic and derisive arguing, and even physical violence. If these behaviors are directed specifically at the stepparent, the joys of parenthood definitely diminish. This doesn't always happen, but be aware that it could.

NEW MARRIAGE, NEW CHILDREN

If your new marriage produces new children, you may encounter even greater complications. Often, new babies bring families closer. But lots of times, stepchildren resent the attention and resources siphoned off by new arrivals.

Regardless of age, all children require—and deserve—a great deal of love and care. But having to deal with antagonistic and destructive behavior by stepchildren will likely eliminate any semblance of normalcy for new children. And, of course, such conflict will severely stress your marriage. The natural mother or father may blame—however inappropriately—the new spouse for some of the stepchild's problems. This only creates more stress. Think about about how you would feel and react in this situation, and whether you even want to risk it.

It May (or May Not) Work

Stepchildren *can* provide an even stronger commitment for newlyweds. Some people just really like raising kids—anyone's kids. The children represent a collective promise and purpose in life. They may bestow great rewards on either or both partners in the new marriage. And they can offer warm and loving relationships and help create a positive, family-oriented life.

Some children warm up to their stepparents, bonding almost the same way they do with biological parents. If one of the natural parents is dead, or is otherwise completely out of the picture, the stepparent may serve as a role model, genuinely filling a void in the child's life. Remember, though: the operative word is *may*.

Unfortunately, predicting the workings of these relationships is, at best, difficult. When children are particularly young, their physiological, psychological, and emotional development is hard to anticipate in any reasonable way. Simply stated, parenthood is a gamble.

> *The Challenge:* Stepchildren Have a Lot to Do with the Marriage's Success
>
> *Making It Work:* Do Your Best to Assess What the Children Are Like; Be Alert to Any Warning Signs

In this sense then, the new marriage is a game of chance for everyone. If the children are into their early teens at the time of the new marriage, you may be able to assess their emotional and psychological states. Somewhat. Use your eyes and your brain. Try not to get overly emotional. Take an objective look at how the children interact, behave, and live. Never assume anything, but don't be afraid to trust your instincts. Any apparent emotional or psychological problems, even in younger children, may be fair warning of problems yet to come. Even if you feel the children will eventually "grow out of it," remember that that can take at least five to ten years.

Hardly anyone is totally well adjusted all the time. Difficult periods crop up for most of us. But when it comes to raising children, situations as well as degrees play especially crucial roles. Things that bother the stepparent may not bother the natural parent; blood ties run deep.

Stress between the stepchildren and the stepparent can manifest itself behaviorally. While many of these behaviors occur between *any* child and natural parent, they can be especially unpleasant for the stepparent. You may think that you won't let things get to you, but real life may not live up to your expectations.

Relations with other family members may even be stressful. Grandparents (and other relatives), for instance, may favor one set of children over the other. They may not care about or even recognize the stepparent's unique challenges.

Still, they can provide support for the stepfamily if they so choose.

Chances are the child may have less remorse about creating tension with the stepparent than with the natural parents. And the stepchild may be far less concerned about or aware of the psychological, emotional, and behavioral ramifications of his or her actions on the stepparent, and on the stepparent's marriage. You simply aren't likely to be as important to the stepchildren as you may wish.

YOUR CHANGED PRIORITIES

When a marriage begins with children, life's priorities change radically—especially when compared to a traditional marriage. Ideally, traditional marriages start with:

- Privacy
- No children
- No stress from children
- No "babysitting" responsibilities
- A honeymoon period

A remarriage may face:

- No privacy or limited privacy
- Immediate child support costs
- Stress from children
- Child-rearing duties
- No honeymoon period

The needs of the children, not the parents, can be the focus of life and the newlywed period may be skipped altogether. Children's needs can douse the fires of marital bliss.

> *The Challenge:* Jumping into Immediate Parenthood
> *Making It Work:* Be Prepared and Willing to Accept the Situation; Try to Get Away Periodically with Your Spouse

Both spouses must accept the lifestyle changes and priorities that are part of the stepfamily package. Even when the children are in the daily care of the natural parent, a lot of issues must be faced. There are no breaks in child-rearing responsibilities and the physical and emotional challenges of marriage become much greater and more immediate than would otherwise be typical. You have to think about whether you can handle this difference, and whether you even want to do so.

A World Without Privacy

For custodial parents, and even non-custodial parents who have children visiting, privacy can become an issue. We all need *some* privacy—even from our own children. But children can be very demanding and, as any responsible parent knows, to bring them up properly, you must attend to their needs.

Quiet evenings of marital bliss, pleasant mornings getting ready for work, and a lot of "down" time during the day can get lost. The lack of privacy may be most noticeable in the evening, but it is always there.

As a stepparent, this may be particularly harsh; someone else's children are impinging on your world. Meanwhile, the natural parent's maternal or paternal instincts may override the problem's significance. The stepparent will need great patience and perseverance to accept this fact. He or she should make time to just be alone or to pursue personal interests and hobbies; it's a good way of coping.

Altered Commitments

In matters of privacy, and in many other matters, the natural parent usually tends to sympathize with the children's needs. We have to expect this from any serious parent. But we also have to expect even more than normal friction between the spouses. And these strains are not one-time occurrences. They can build over the years, creating their own pressures to add to the pressures of everyday life.

A QUICK SURPRISE

Alma Torrance married early in life—the first time, anyway. By the time she divorced George at 23, she had two small children. Amy was two and Jonathan was four when their parents called it quits; they simply couldn't get along. Shortly after the divorce, George was in a serious automobile accident and died within a few weeks of complications from internal injuries.

Soon after, Alma met Albert. Although she had vowed never to marry again, true love intervened, and the wedding was on.

Unfortunately, Alma became seriously ill within days of marriage. She developed complications from Lyme disease, and the combination of arthritis and other problems landed her in and out of bed for nearly a year.

Albert rose to the occasion. He took care of Amy and Jonathan, the house, the cat and dog, and held down a job delivering fuel oil to residential customers. Fortunately, Alma's mother lived nearby and was able to lend a hand. During that difficult year, with no extra time or money, Albert really learned to appreciate what it takes to look after two children.

> *When Alma finally recovered, she and Albert waited a couple of years to have a child of their own. They agreed to share the work, with Alma taking care of their children and the home. And Albert was happy about that!*

> *The Challenge:* Commitment to Prior Children May Seem to Diminish Commitment to the New Spouse
> *Making It Work:* Constant and Sincere Commitment to the New Spouse and Marriage Is Absolutely Essential

The presence of stepchildren will color all of your decisions. Whether you're dealing with financial issues, social concerns, or other matters, certain pressures and conflicts are inherent when you have someone else's child around. While a traditional marriage allows for common goals, stepfamilies force parents to consider the needs of a whole additional group of people. Thus, the potential for conflict is greater. This doesn't mean the situation is impossible, but the challenges are significant.

A Constant Barrage

As discussed earlier, children are naturally demanding and their demands cannot easily be ignored. Further, natural parents are unlikely to overlook their own children's needs, and if they did, you probably would lose some respect for them.

Of course, there are great differences in children's behaviors. Generalization is nearly impossible. Some children are easy to deal with. Others are exasperating.

> *The Challenge:* Dealing with Annoying Stepchildren
> *Making It Work:* Know Your Limits

As children become teenagers, they may become more carefree and lackadaisical. Again, not all teenagers, but many, follow this pattern. Sometimes these attitudes seep into their adult lives. Stepparents may have trouble coping with some of the rather mundane, but very noticeable, changes. For example, the teenager may be messy, while the stepparent is neat and orderly. Constant fighting over these little issues can be tiring.

Indeed, behavior that merely irritates a natural parent may drive a stepparent crazy. Children (and especially teenagers) may like loud music, blaring television sets, or the racket of drum practice. While messiness and noise are hardly unusual teenage and young adult pastimes, prospective stepparents should be prepared. Will these things constantly bother you?

Other behaviors, sometimes symptoms of underlying psychological problems, may cause even more stress. Anger, for instance, may be expressed through short-temperedness. Anger directed toward the stepparent as a result of the psychological impact of the divorce, as mentioned previously, is common and can get pretty rough. This can last well into adulthood. Are you ready to cope with this?

Tempers can flare into physical violence. Criminal behavior is not unknown. Like adults, many children are pleasant and sweet; others are not. When they are little, you may see adorable bundles of warmth. But as they grow, so do their personalities and behaviors. *The stepparent is particularly vulnerable as a target of anger.*

Fortunately, children can outgrow destructive behaviors. Unfortunately, the maturing process may take a great deal of time. Meanwhile, the stepparent's life can be woeful. If the stepparent is in the custodial family, every day can be a trial.

> *The Challenge:* Tolerating It All
> *Making It Work:* Determine Your Threshhold for Stress

While it is pretty difficult to predict behavior, it is still a concern that should be understood by any prospective stepparent. Carefully assess your own tolerance for people and problems, and the strength of your pending marriage. By examining your *own* stress points, flexibility, and tolerance-levels, you can at least gauge your possible actions and reactions.

On a really practical level, consider the mundane issues. Who does the laundry for the stepchildren? Who cooks and cleans for them? Little things add up quickly. Chores can be discussed and divided up in family meetings and informal discussions. But will the child and the natural parents follow through? Will the stepparent be left holding the bag?

YOU WANT IT YOUR WAY

Having children means compromise. You set the rules, and they ignore or change them. You want the door closed; they open it. You want the lights turned off to save energy; they habitually leave them on. You like the kitchen left clean; they leave a mess.

A child may test a stepparent's tolerance more frequently than a natural parent's. And each of us has a different threshold—a willingness and an ability—to accept certain behaviors. Depending on your relationship with each stepchild, your own threshold may vary. As a stepparent, you will have to cope with everyday dilemmas, and possibly with fewer long-term rewards. This may be difficult for some people to accept.

A VIOLENT REACTION

Growing up in a middle-class Cleveland family, Alan Slopes never had much exposure to family violence. But a few years after marrying Thelma Young he got a bitter taste.

Thelma had two teenagers—Al, aged 14, and Bob, aged 16—when she married Alan. By that time, she and the boys were pretty independent. The natural father was never a great influence and quickly faded from the picture. Alan stepped in thinking that the two teenaged boys would benefit from a little discipline and a father figure. He was dead wrong.

After about six months, the teenagers became noticeably more difficult to handle. Both, but especially the older boy, began talking back more and threatening Alan. Finally, less than a year after the wedding, Bob exploded; he had had a long and loud argument with Alan. He kicked in two doors in the house and broke a window as he threw a telephone at his stepfather.

After Bob stormed off, Alan realized that things were never good and were getting worse. He thought about seeking family counseling but finally decided that he had only one choice: divorce. Eventually Thelma agreed that there was no hope for their marriage, and they broke up.

The Challenge: Disciplining Stepchildren
Making It Work: Let the Natural Parent Do It When Possible

As with any child, when a stepchild doesn't obey, it's time for discipline. *Disciplining someone else's child is extremely difficult.* Frequently the child doesn't view the stepparent as an authority figure. To complicate matters, a child may use the stepparent as a psychological punching bag, taking out anger from their parents' divorce on the "newcomer." The natural parent may not back you. What's more, disciplining children successfully means setting rules early on, but the stepparent probably wasn't around early on. This can make the situation even more challenging.

A Few Other Concerns

Children inevitably come with friends. Your house may be occupied from time to time by various people who are not of your own choosing. As the child blossoms into a teenager, boyfriends and girlfriends will populate the realm. You may lose control over the use of your telephone and maybe even your refrigerator. At times, it may seem as if you're feeding the whole neighborhood.

Stepparents may also have to deal with the stepchildren's sexual behavior and activities. And they may be unpleasant dealings. Chapter 5 discusses some of these complications further. Depending upon the scenerio and the characters involved, such matters may be thrust entirely upon you. Can you deal with these situations in a constructive and supportive way?

All manner of life's problems can occur as the child grows. In a custodial household, you as stepparent cannot avoid most of these issues and events. The natural parents may not assume their full share of responsibility.

> *The Challenge:* The Rewards of Being a Stepparent May Be Limited
> *Making It Work:* Be Very Realistic in Your Expectations

Your hard work may not always be rewarded by your stepchildren. Often they don't express thanks, and many parents may not expect them to. Usually, natural parents assume that their children love and appreciate them. Stepparents, on the other hand, may have a more difficult time accepting this apparent lack of appreciation—especially when they feel that they have gone beyond the call of duty to help rear someone else's children. *The stepparent's expectations may be unrealistic.* Certainly not *all* stepchildren are ungrateful, but many are. While you may get some thanks, don't expect any. Even your spouse may not thank you!

Still more troublesome is having the other natural parent walk into the picture and end up winning your stepchildren's devotion. This may be especially hard to take after you have spent years rearing their children.

It is not all that unusual for a natural parent to enter the picture after his or her children have grown up—when the child-rearing work is done. They "claim" back the children emotionally. This can be even more irksome if the natural parent had also refused to provide the children with financial support. Knowingly or unknowingly, the natural parent can play on the child's emotions, making things unpleasant. After all this, the stepparent may resent seeing the children re-bond with the natural parent, sometimes rejecting the "outsider" who helped raise them. You have to be prepared to accept this possibility.

Don't necessarily plan on a long-term commitment. Although many stepchildren hold their stepparents in as much regard as their natural parents, others do not. Regardless of past experiences—even painful experiences—some revert to the natural parent's biological hold. If the children are older at the time of the remarriage, they are less likely to bond with the stepparent.

THE REWARDS

Great rewards can come from rearing someone else's children. Many stepparents will see the payoffs of parenthood as they see their stepchildren grow and thrive. Helping to educate and mold a child into an adult can be one of life's greatest accomplishments. *Any* parent can attest to that.

Even the trials of parenthood bring tremendous dividends. For stepparents who establish and maintain loving relationships with their stepchildren, the rewards are abundant; their stepchildren are no different from natural children.

Consider everything that can go wrong, but also consider everything that can go *right*. The last chapter of this book has more information and thoughts on what to do and how to try to make things even better.

A SHORT REPAYMENT INTERVAL

Howard Sunderland always felt that he was a great father, not only to his own two children from his successful marriage to Alice Silton, but also to the two children from her first marriage. Her children were eight and ten when she remarried.

Alice's first husband was, by any measure, a louse. He never helped with the children during the marriage, nor did he do anything after the divorce. He failed to provide child support, and he even refused to talk to the children at all for about eight years while they were growing up.

All of a sudden, when the children were in college (for which their natural father refused to pay his share) this guy resurfaced. He started communicating with the children, inviting them to visit and acting as though nothing had gone wrong. He still refused to pay for anything, but he was back in the picture, playing the part of the caring father.

The children responded by warming up to him and distancing themselves from Howard. They communicated well with their mother but made it clear who "Dad" was in their eyes.

Howard had a hard time accepting all of this. Finally he realized that fighting it would be futile and he remained cordial to the stepchildren. But their relationship never improved. His resentment never went away.

5

Beyond the Challenge: More Complexity

By now you should know that being a stepparent isn't easy. But wait: it can get even more complicated. All kinds of differences between you and your stepchildren and your spouse can lead to tremendous conflict and stress. The most important thing you can do to ward off potential problems is to be aware of them.

While "traditional" intact families have their share of troubles, there's a certain naturalness to them. Stepfamilies, on the other hand, live in a kind of forced situation, a situation that can present astounding complexities and often, a greater potential for failure. This doesn't mean that all is hopeless, but only that the challenges are significant.

This chapter talks about going beyond normal complexity and facing some of the ultimate problems that can compound things.

Some of these ultimate situations, perhaps most of them, would be challenging for *any* marriage. They are likely to add to the problems and stresses of remarriages. Yet for some people and in some circumstances, more strains may offer more opportunity for cooperation and caring. In other families, however, they may make the marriage unworkable.

But in all of these different situations, there remains a common thread: all parties in the marriage must put forth extra efforts. Even for a strong, vibrant marriage—one not deeply affected by these issues—the partners may need extra strength within and between themselves to cope with external pressures from a society that is often either uncaring or unsympathetic.

MIXING RELIGIONS

More than ever, we are seeing marriages where the husband and wife come from different religious backgrounds. Loosening of family ties, increasing mobility and mixing in our society, opening up to other people's views and perspectives, and other influences in the great melting pot that have characterized the United States in this century have made religiously-mixed marriages nearly inevitable.

Further, aside from the flourishing number of religions represented in our nation, the varying philosophies and sects within any one religion reinforce this marital trend. And on an individual level, it's a trend that can lead to problems. For instance, a husband and wife can be from the same religion, and even hold many similar philosophical attitudes. But if one spouse is more observant, or even more active in his or her religious community, this alone can create friction. Indeed, marriage and religious conflict doesn't mix particularly well.

The Challenge: Religious Differences Can Add Extra Difficulty to Marriages
Making It Work: Work Out Religious Practices Before the Marriage

When it comes to stepfamilies, religious differences can lead to even greater stresses. In a traditional marriage, this dilemma needs to be resolved initially so that each spouse can practice his or her own religion as he or she sees fit. But when children are already in the scene, the picture becomes more complicated; some agreement must be reached about which—if any—religion the children will be brought up in and how that will be accomplished. In a stepfamily, this issue must be solved almost instantaneously—and since the children are likely already observing the natural parent's religion, the stepparent must be willing to accept this.

Sometimes one spouse will convert to the religion of the other spouse, perhaps solving the problem. Oftentimes, however, children are brought up without a religious orientation or philosophy, or they follow the beliefs of the more insistent or dominant spouse.

Religious dissension and disparity can be particularly acute during the holidays. For example, since Christmas is not a Jewish holiday, a non-Jewish spouse may be upset over his or her partner's lack of enthusiasm for the season. People can sometimes be insensitive to the religious beliefs and thoughts of their spouses, particularly when there are fundamental differences. This is something that some Americans give little thought to.

If the stepchildren of one spouse are being brought up in one religion, it doesn't necessarily mean that children born into the new union will be brought up likewise. Again, this is a time for discussion and negotiation. Even so, a religiously-dominant spouse may insist that the children follow his or her beliefs. Of course, as the children grow, they may develop their own ideas and preferences—preferences which can disconcert both parents.

Another consideration is that religious differences can turn into problems if one spouse wants to commit considerable time and effort to his or her religion and the other does not. This conflict may become even worse if the stepchildren are involved in religious training and activities that call for parental commitment of time and effort.

Also, like many things in life, religious adherence may also require financial commitments. With all of the other economic burdens placed on stepparents, giving money to support even worthy religious goals may strain the marriage more.

Religious education and training, as well as various ceremonies and rites of passage, may end up as both an emotional and a financial imposition on at least one of the parents. And a parent who wants to send the children or stepchildren to a parochial school may clash with the desires of the other parent.

On the other hand, religious involvement can be a great source of both emotional and marital support. Religion can strengthen families in general, and stepfamilies in particular, especially where family values and interpersonal communications are concerned.

The Challenge: Religious Differences Need to Be Addressed

Making It Work: Focus on Using Religion in Positive Ways to Strengthen the Marriage and to Instill Values in the Children

For many Americans, religious values and practice serve a tremendously valuable role in daily life. Religion can be a great stabilizing force in family life and can greatly strengthen the stepfamily. Conversely, religious differences that become an issue in the marriage can be a further, and significant, source of stress.

It is vitally important to discuss and carefully work out religious issues prior to any marriage. But for the stepfamily, these issues are even more critical.

If it is at all possible, take advantage of the tremendous family guidance and counseling role that religion and religious leaders can play. These resources can strengthen the stepfamily and improve everyone's commitment to one another and to the family in general.

At the very least, try to be *sure* that religious differences will not further compound an already complex situation to such an extent that the marriage itself is called into question. As with the many other issues that stepfamilies face, the only real way to address religious differences is through *honest, open, and frank communication*. And a little prayer can't hurt, either.

MIXED SIGNALS AT CHRISTMAS

Jackie Wren's marriage was tragically cut short by the death of her husband Bob. Bob and Jackie were both nonpracticing Catholics. Still, Jackie had always felt that the Christian holidays were important—especially Christmas. She also wanted her three-year-old son, A.J., to be brought up a Catholic, and maybe even go to private Catholic schools, as she had done.

Then Jackie met Mark Silverstein at work. Immediately, they both knew that they had a lot in common, except for one thing—religion. Mark was Jewish. While he wasn't particularly observant, he certainly identified with his religion and wanted his children brought up as Jews.

As Christmas approached, the religious differences between Jackie and Mark became more and more apparent. Mark seemed to have little interest in preparing for Christmas and clearly wasn't very enthusiastic. After all, it wasn't his holiday. Jackie wanted an exciting Christmas for her son, who was now aware that Santa Claus brought gifts for well-behaved children.

Finally, the tension became unbearable. Jackie and Mark had it out. She accused him of not being interested in Christmas and of spoiling the holiday for her son. Mark could bear the pressure no more, and tried to explain carefully to Jackie that Christmas was neither part of his background nor his beliefs. He started off a little bit sarcastically, but eventually cooled off, and when they had a frank conversation, it became clear to both Jackie and Mark that their religious differences were just too great for the relationship to go much further. They did remain friends, however.

DIFFERENCES OF RACE AND ETHNICITY

Chances are, ethnically and racially mixed couples who are already on their way to the marriage altar have already largely resolved those differences for themselves. Still, when it comes to stepfamilies, racial and ethnic differences need special consideration.

As a general rule, ethnic differences are less likely to be of importance than racial differences. Even so, with the considerable ethnic strife throughout the world today, and the world's history of ethnic intolerance, it is vital for couples from different backgrounds to be doubly sure that their upbringings will not inhibit happiness. When children are involved, the stepparent must be confident that he or she harbors no overt, or even hidden, prejudices that could hurt the family.

Differences in diet and nutrition, food preferences, physical appearance, and dress are an outgrowth of ethnic differences. And indirectly, they can spark friction. Philosophies can crash head-on on a whole range of issues, such as health care, child-rearing, the roles of husbands and wives, money, and other basic, but often taken for granted, matters in everyday life. And when stepchildren are brought into a marriage, these differences can affect the natural parent's and stepparent's relationships with the children.

The Challenge: Ethnic and Cultural Differences Can Create Additional Problems

Making It Work: Be Sure that Any Prejudices or Even Cultural and Philosophical Differences Related to Ethnic and Racial Factors Have Been Thought Through, Discussed, and Worked Out

For some, it is often difficult to fully recognize and openly discuss the implications of ethnic differences. These differences fundamentally relate to attitudes, philosophies, and behaviors. Even attitudes of other family members, such as in-laws, can spring from ethnic backgrounds and upbringings. Their interactions with the stepparent, their expectations, and their thoughts about the children will be shaped by these inbred factors.

Despite our society's self-image of being "sophisticated," racial intermarriage is difficult for people to accept. The good news is that racial differences aren't likely to cause significant problems for a stable, happy couple. Obviously, both husband and wife should understand, and be prepared to cope with, reactions from certain segments of our society toward interracial marriage. Attitudes toward the children of these marriages and toward any stepchildren brought into the marriage are especially relevant.

And then there's the issue of the stepchildren's racial identity. According to Dr. Fredi Schwebel of New York City's Center for Marital and Family Therapy, one of the best ways to for a stepparent to deal with a child from a different race is to spend as much time together as possible—before getting married. Learn as much as you can about his or her heritage including everyday things such as tastes in food, music, and dress.

For instance, what if your four-year-old stepson wants plantains for dinner and you've never heard of plantains? Even if he tells you that they look like green bananas, you can't simply hand him a green banana and expect him to be satisfied. So always be curious, tactful, and respectful.

Also, seemingly subtle qualities that we tend to take for granted such as a person's sense of humor can have cultural influences. What you think is funny may very well offend your stepchild. In other words, you can hardly begin to prepare for your new life if you haven't prepared yourself for its details.

Another thing to watch out for is the way a child from another culture expresses him or herself and relates to others. It may be quite different than what you're used to—and it's crucial not to misinterpret these differences. A quiet child may be mistaken as a cold child rather than a respectful one.

Again, Dr. Schwebel emphasizes that stepparents must

spend a great deal of time getting to know their new family before making everything official.

DIFFERENCES IN LIFESTYLE PREFERENCES

The pressures of rearing stepchildren can also be exacerbated by other differences between the parents. Differences in philosophies regarding the accumulation and spending of money, lifestyle preferences, and entertainment and relaxation tastes can often create marital stress. And when it comes to raising either stepchildren or biological children, marital stress doesn't help. Indeed, more differences can make everything more difficult to deal with.

A FEW OTHER DISCREET ISSUES

Sexual molestation is an increasingly common undercurrent in our society today. The media have raised public awareness regarding the extent and seriousness of this problem through increased coverage. Government and judicial activism has resulted in a more aggressive stance by social service agencies and the legal system in dealing with these matters. This awakening has had many positive results in redressing this important national problem.

At the same time, accusations of molestation can be used by people as a form of revenge. This matter is especially sensitive for those whose stepchildren express their anger at their parents' divorce, at family violence, and at unwanted remarriages; they can falsely accuse the stepparent of sexual advances and mistreatment. Indeed, stepparents are particularly susceptible to such accusations or even to threats of accusations.

This is an extremely complex and sensitive situation, given the need to deal with actual criminal behavior while at the same time protecting those who are falsely accused. The private nature of such terrible acts, and the multitude of emotional and psychological currents they involve, make it much more difficult to resolve problems easily and fairly.

When stepparents are accused of sexual molestation, aggressive social and legal intervention is warranted. Just the same, the protection of individual reputations and the preservation of the family is vital. False accusations can cause irreparable damage to the family, which may be the child's objective.

Repairing the emotional damage that results from even the *hint* of this type of maltreatment is a true challenge. *Professional counseling is essential.* Stepparents and their spouses must address these issues aggressively and rapidly, determine the truth, and resolve the underlying problems. If and when the accusations are firmly established to be false, immediate family therapy as well as therapy for the accusing child is very important. The causes of false accusations can usually be determined by professionals. Ultimately, stepparents must be aware of any potential for such allegations and try to avoid situations where any conduct could even remotely be misconstrued. Finally, open discussions between the spouses are also a must.

Another complication: drug and alcohol abuse. Besides, of course, the misuse of illicit drugs and all forms of alcohol, the problem also includes misuse of prescription drugs, and nicotine, a highly addictive drug.

Abuse affects the family's behavior and emotions. It hurts interpersonal relationships, distorts behavior, can lead to personality disorders, causes physical problems, can be a drain on a family's already strained finances, and can wreak havoc in many other ways. Secondhand smoke can forever damage the health of non-smokers. Drug and alcohol abuse can lead to physical violence.

All of this speaks again to the need for rapid intervention and to the importance of a cohesive, family-oriented approach to finding solutions. Mix drug and alcohol abuse with the fragile environment of the stepfamily and you can expect the deterioration of the family.

CONCLUDING COMMENTS

The complexities of stepfamilies—even in the best of circumstances—is a real challenge to the newly married couple. Add in difficulties with finances, former spouses, juvenile personalities, and developmental disorders, and the challenge escalates. Add to the map the types of extremely intricate and potentially difficult situations described in this chapter, and your road ahead may seem truly unmaneuverable.

Remember though, you *do* have options, and there is always help. These problems do not need to be, and probably cannot be, solved without professional help, so take advantage of the excellent counseling and intervention programs available in most cities nationwide. Work hard and aggressively to solve any underlying problems and then to strengthen the marriage itself. No matter how impossible the obstacles may seem, there is always hope.

Part Three

The Other People

6

Can the New Marriage and Family Survive?

Every marriage faces tensions. Even in the best of situations, life is challenging. And stepchildren will challenge a marriage even more. The ultimate question of course is: can the new marriage survive?

> *The Challenge:* The New Marriage May Be Constantly Stressed and Tested
>
> *Making It Work:* Everyone Has to Work Hard at Enhancing the Marriage, and with Real Commitment

Marriages with underlying instability or incompatibility can be pushed over the brink. When it comes to stepfamilies, constant, day-to-day pressures from the children and even from the former spouse can build. Conflict, discontent, and disagreement may become the norm!

THE NEW SPOUSE IS IMPORTANT

Whether the natural parent places the new union and the new spouse as the top priority says a lot about the likelihood of marital success. Hardly anyone wants to play second fiddle for their entire married lives to someone else's children. *If the marriage itself isn't a top priority, then a rocky road lies ahead.*

This is not to say that the children should be ignored or treated improperly. Rather, the stepparent must be given top priority. This is difficult for most natural parents and especially for those with vibrant parental instincts. Possible guilt over his or her divorce may make things even worse. The need for balance in setting priorities lasts forever.

To guard against failure, any marriage must be based on a clear, mutual agreement over priorities. It takes a sense of mission, an understanding of each other's perspectives, and constant vigilance to alleviate, or at least to accommodate, the strains that children can bring. While these principles are important for any family, they are far more pressing when stepchildren are involved.

Ignoring these basic concepts may doom your marriage. Children from previous marriages skew the normalcy of new marriages beyond any recognition and create tremendous pressures that must be accommodated.

In this day and age, marriages risk failure from day one. They also strive for success. But a successful marriage *must be earned.* Inability to recognize and deal with the added pressures of stepchildren may lead to divorce, hardship for one or both spouses, or a bad environment for the children. At worst, it can lead to all of the above.

To review some key principles:

- Make the marriage the number-one priority.
- Agree on other priorities.
- Seek common goals.
- Be sensitive to each other's needs and feelings.
- Support each other.
- Identify problems and seek solutions.
- Don't let problems with the former spouse damage the new marriage.

THE EMOTIONAL EFFORT

It doesn't take a Dr. Spock to figure out that children compete for their parents' attention. They need an almost bottomless reservoir of their parents' emotional and psychological attention and support.

The Challenge: Stepchildren versus New Children
Making It Work: Handle Everyone with Care

Sibling rivalry is normal in every family. Just think back to your own childhood. If you have brothers or sisters, you'll probably remember having fights. Little matters such as who got the most chocolate pudding for dessert could erupt into family civil wars. So where stepchildren versus "new" children are concerned, you can pretty much count on rivalry.

Just the same, it's a different sort of rivalry, a rivalry that is based on family history. That is, stepchildren may suddenly feel displaced by new arrivals. They can lose their status as the only girl or the only boy in the family, or as the youngest or the only child. And as they lose their status, they can lose their "perks": complete attention, privacy, and even material possessions; parents usually encourage siblings to share toys and the like with each other. Even if the stepchildren live with the former spouse, you can expect a certain, albeit lesser, degree of jealousy and animosity. Over time, however, stepsiblings can develop close bonds, and occasionally, even bonds that are stronger than those with their own sisters and brothers.

In the meantime, you can take some practical steps to create harmony, or at the very least, to reduce tensions. To begin, openly discuss the situation with your spouse. It's not possible, fair, or realistic for one parent to deal with the problem single-handedly.

Together, recognize one of life's most precious resources: time. Use it with great care. Try to do as much as possible as a family and by the same token, make sure that each of the children gets an equal amount of attention. Also, despite your own natural urges to favor your own children, treat everyone with the same rules, the same sense of respect, the same sense of care, and the same sense of belonging. Encourage grandparents, aunts, uncles, and friends to do likewise.

Another good idea for stepsiblings who are close in age is to encourage them to work on a project together. Making pancakes for Sunday breakfast, painting a mural for the family room, building a snowman or a sandcastle, or whatever can teach them cooperation and give them an opportunity to have fun together and get to know each other better.

When children do have small disputes, let them work it out for themselves; unless there's a real battle going on, your intervention could be interpreted as favoritism.

THE COMPETITION FOR AFFECTION

Betsy and Harry Larsen thought everything was going great. Harry's child from his previous marriage, Anne, was doing well in the new family, and at age seven seemed to have survived the death of her mother. Anne got along very well with Betsy. And three years after Betsy and Harry's marriage, she seemed really excited about the arrival of her new stepsister, Loren. Anne helped, in her way, to take care of the baby.

In later months, however, as the baby grew and became more playful and interesting, Anne became withdrawn and argumentative. She was especially angry with her father, and she barely talked to Betsy.

Fearing some serious medical problem, the Larsens took Anne to a pediatrician. Physically, everything checked out fine. But with a little prodding, the doctor was able to discern that Anne was very disturbed by all of the attention that Loren was getting. Some counseling by the doctor helped the Larsens realize that they had been lavishing attention on Loren and, at least compared to a year earlier, they were ignoring Anne.

After some weeks of psychological reinforcement, things improved but never quite got back to the way they had been, and Anne's relationship with Betsy seemed strained from then on.

THE IN-LAWS

As discussed previously, the in-laws, grandparents, and other relatives must be supportive of the new marriage and of the stepparent. Still, they may be unhappy about the divorce, or they may not like the new spouse or the way the stepparent relates to the stepchildren. In this case, they can be another source of stress. If they are not going to help, consider telling them—gently—to keep out of the way.

THE BOTTOM LINE

The bottom line is that children from previous marriages dilute the resources available for the marriage and for any new children. Financial, social, emotional, and other family resources will be spread thinner. There are some potential benefits for your new children from having older stepbrothers and stepsisters. But these come with a price.

Of course it is impossible to predict if the new marriage can survive. It won't be easy. But it is definitely possible. The last chapter of this book provides help in mapping a road to success.

7

The Ex-Spouse

Let's start with the previous marriage and the ex-spouse. If the couple was so wonderful together, you probably wouldn't be in the picture at all. For that matter, a potential stepparent had better look at his or her future spouse and ask why the previous marriage failed. And from a practical point of view, a former spouse is still another person who must be dealt with. Some former spouses *do* remain best friends, though this is hardly the norm.

When former spouses can remain friends, chances are that there will be fewer problems with stepchildren and that the problems that do crop up will be far more manageable for you. Remember, though, when such friendships do survive divorce, they have to endure for a long time and may have to face many difficult issues.

Then there are former couples who aren't on the best of terms, but who are still committed to their children and are mature enough to work out the responsibilities of parenthood together.

If your spouse's "ex" turns out to be responsible, helpful, and even friendly, be thankful. But if this isn't the case—and quite often it isn't—be alert to potential problems and try to solve them early on.

WHO IS RESPONSIBLE?

Joint custody is a rather impractical concept in most divorces. *Whoever has the children living with them every week, all the time, are the ones really responsible.* The former spouse may assume some burdens, but the ultimate responsibility lies with whomever lives with the child. And this means that the stepparent will fully share that responsibility. This situation may be aggravated by having to deal with the former spouse.

WHO COMES FIRST?

If you marry someone with children, your spouse will naturally have great regard for you; many people aren't willing to become instant parents. At the same time, your spouse's natural concerns for his or her children will impinge on your marriage.

Divorce is an especially cruel reality for children. Of course, if your spouse's previous marriage was emotionally rocky, violent, nonsupportive or otherwise destructive, divorce may have been the lesser of two evils. Many parents try to minimize the divorce's effect on their children by forcing themselves to be cordial to each other. The idea is to not alienate the children any further with divisive behavior.

This is a charade of the natural parents' relationship, making the stepparent pretend that everything is rosy. The new spouse may go along with the act, playing a role that he or she is uncomfortable with while resenting or just disliking the former spouse.

As time passes, the real picture will become clear; children see through just about everything. Even so, this charade *may* last long enough to dampen the divorce's emotional effects on the children.

Still, the emotional effects can be profound. Parents who use their children as pawns to get back at their former mate end up hurting the children more than anyone else. An ex-husband or ex-wife who understands this and who can rise above his or her hostilities toward a former mate will make life better for everyone.

THE DATING GAME

Mary Elizabeth Adams was thrilled to meet John Thomas. Both were in their late forties, and both had a child from a previous marriage. Mary Elizabeth felt that she and John were compatible in virtually every respect, including their prior marital experiences. She also felt that since their two children were about the same age, they might get along well and that there would not be any great long-term difficulties dealing with child-rearing and such matters.

But she was shocked when she first met John's daughter Valerie. Mary Elizabeth had gone over to John's house for dinner one night after they had been seeing each other for about a month. The idea of course was that the dinner would be an opportunity for her to meet and get to know Valerie a little bit.

Unfortunately, John's daughter was extremely antagonistic and rebellious toward Mary Elizabeth. During dinner, which Valerie initially refused to attend, she made numerous derogatory comments about Mary Elizabeth, picking on her taste in clothing and her political views. By the end of the evening,

Mary Elizabeth was herself totally turned off and disturbed by the whole experience.

After going home and thinking about things for a little while, she finally concluded that the situation was basically hopeless. She felt that even if she made a concerted effort to win over Valerie, the likelihood of succeeding was not great. And John himself had warned her that Valerie was somewhat disturbed as a result of the divorce and was antagonistic to other women that John invited over. Finally Mary Elizabeth decided that she didn't need the mental anguish of dealing with the whole situation, and she never went out with John again.

HOW TO DEAL WITH THE EX-SPOUSE

Where feasible, an intelligent and rational relationship between the natural parents makes managing practical matters easier. The divorce decree and associated court orders, as well as any other agreements worked out during the divorce settlement, is the basis for making decisions about the stepchildren. Unfortunately, especially if the children are young, the divorce agreements are unlikely to anticipate everything that can happen over the next fifteen or twenty years. Can *anyone* really plan for *every* contingency yet to come?

Major issues, such as paying for college, may be left largely unresolved. The natural parents may need to go back to court for amendments to the original decree or informally work out solutions to additional problems as they occur. When one of the natural parents is no longer alive, or disavows any involvement with the children, decision-making is obviously simplified. In this situation, a deceased parent may have left an estate that is managed in trust for the children by a third party.

The Difficult Arrangements

Dealing with the former spouse may require complex, and sometimes expensive, arrangements. Deciding who has the children at any point in time, how to get them from one home to another, who handles the children's social and educational calendars, and the other mundane details of daily life have to be worked out with yet another person. This complicated planning only adds to an already harried existence.

The Challenge: Dealing with an Obstructive Former Spouse

Making It Work: Use Aggressive Tactics in the Divorce Agreement; Be Forthright and Demanding from Then On

---

The other spouse may not cooperate and may even hinder things simply to make your life difficult. The ex-husband or wife may not be very reliable, either, and fail to follow through with commitments. Sharing of expenses such as child care, transportation, and other needs may not be fair.

Naturally, all of this can create stress for the new stepparent. In short, a vengeful ex-spouse may:

- Not assume financial, social, logistic, or emotional responsibility
- Play psychological games with the children
- Be antagonistic and abusive
- Refuse to cooperate in all arrangements
- Be irresponsible

Regardless of who has physical custody of the children, life will be more complex, difficult, and expensive while each former spouse tries to create a new life for himself or herself—a difficult enough task for anyone.

Being Mean

Aside from the above-mentioned problems, you may have to contend with basic harassment. Generally former spouses have trouble getting along. When children are involved, even more opportunities come up for harassing a former spouse. For example, a natural parent may play the children off against the other parent or stepparent.

More subtle psychological warfare is also common. Guerilla tactics can range from feeding lies to the children, a common ploy, to threatening legal action of various sorts. People's abilities to be obnoxious to each other is limited only by the human imagination.

At the extreme, there could be threats of violence. The legal system is remarkably unresponsive to the needs of couples in conflict; our nation's track record on family violence ranks as a major tragedy and disgrace.

Nasty behavior may extend to other family members, such as grandparents and cousins. They may even actively participate in the tactical warfare. Remaining friendly with former relatives may be so difficult that the effort isn't worth it.

Retribution, hatred, dislike, resentment, and other emotions are common in divorce. Men are probably more likely than women to be disagreeable, although there is no firm data on this. Still, regardless of gender, hostilities may be played out in many ways and all will stress the new marriage and taint the lives of the children.

Your spouse may be angered and even bewildered by

being caught in the middle of all of this. A difficult former spouse may be hard to accept and this can create tension in the new marriage that is hard to dissipate.

The Challenge: Stepparenting When a Natural Parent Has Died
Making It Work: Help the Children Accept and Cope with the Death

Of course, some remarriages with children occur after the death of a spouse. The couple may have been happily married, or the death may have occurred after the divorce. In either case, expect your stepchild to be somewhat devastated; the death of a parent is difficult for any normal person to deal with at any age. All kinds of feelings can come up including despair, anger, resentment, fear, and a sense of abandonment. Also, a parent is sometimes more revered after death than during life. So unless your stepchild is unusually well adjusted, the death of his or her parent is likely to present problems.

Don't let the former spouse be a ghost haunting your marriage. Allowing that to happen can only hurt your stepchild, your spouse, and you. Keep in mind that you can never replace nor live up to a child's image of his or her deceased parent, so don't even try. What you can do is to be supportive and help to create an atmosphere in which the family deals with—but does not dwell on—the situation. But be careful not to rush your stepchild. Grieving is a natural part of the acceptance process and acceptance of the death, as well as acceptance of you, takes time.

If the child is unable to cope despite your efforts, professional counseling—family, individual, or a combination—may be valuable. Sometimes frictions develop between a child who has lost a parent to death and his or her stepparent. And your spouse can't and shouldn't try to referee. After all, he or she has also suffered a loss and has memories, and perhaps, unresolved feelings.

How much time should your stepchild devote to therapy? It depends. Factors such as the length of time that has elapsed since the death and the child's personality are variables. In some cases, short-term therapy may do the job. In other cases, it may take years. Be patient.

AWAY WE GO

Today's economic uncertainty and people's great mobility makes it common for one parent to eventually move away. Sometimes both parents leave their previous residences. Job changes, remarriages, and the psychological need for change can lead to relocation.

This is a serious concern for everyone. If a parent moves a good distance away from his or her children, expect added expenses and logistic hassles from arranging for visitation trips.

The Challenge: Moving Away from the Other Parent
Making It Work: Get Everyone on Board; Arrange the Long-Term Details in Advance

For the custodial parent, relocating means uprooting the children once again. Arranging for visits can become a big issue. Sometimes one parent will move solely to make life more difficult for the other parent. If this is the case, he or she will do even less of the child-rearing, and an out-of-sight, out-of-mind philosophy could spell less financial and emotional commitment.

Occasionally a custodial parent is shocked to find that when he or she moves, a child doesn't want to go along and instead stays with the other parent. It may be difficult to go against these wishes. Depending on the child's age and the court's divorce decree, a parent may lose custody by moving. This can also lead to more dissension between the natural parents and greater stress for the stepparent. On the other hand, if relations between the natural parents are not good to begin with, a move can reduce interaction.

Be careful to weigh the costs and benefits of relocating. Jobs and overall economic considerations can be pretty important and may even override more practical issues. Also, the many stresses involved in divorce may mean that relocating can actually *improve* the children's lives in the long run.

Whatever the outcome, the stepparent may be caught in the middle. If a stepfamily is uprooted because the stepparent has accepted a job in another city, he or she may be "blamed" for the situation.

CAN WE MOVE?

Alan Fisch learned firsthand how the courts can intervene in life's decisions. For a variety of reasons, mostly due to Margaret's alcoholism, the court had awarded Alan full custody of Bobby and allowed his mother weekly visits. But a provision of Alan's divorce decree stipulated that he must remain within twenty miles of his residence to make those visits easier.

Then Alan's employer presented him with a great job opportunity. However, he would have to relocate to another city 1,500 miles away. A 40 percent pay boost, lots of perks, and a fast track up the company ladder would all be his. Alan's lawyer recommended that they ask the court to modify the divorce decree so that Alan could legally move.

Originally Alan had agreed to this provision to facilitate the divorce and also because he never expected such a fine opportunity at work. He would never have agreed to give up custody of Bobby, especially with Margaret's problems. And after reading about conflicting court decisions in different jurisdictions, he was a little apprehensive.

Even knowing the risks, he was still shocked when the court denied his petition. Margaret had obtained very competent counsel, and the court held that the move would unreasonably restrict her opportunities for visits with Bobby. The court told Alan that if he wanted to move he would have to give custody of Bobby to his ex-wife. Devastated and bitter, Alan turned down the promotion.

WHEN TO WORRY

Of course, one parent has the child living with him or her, and the other does not. When the child lives with the other spouse, you have a different array of concerns. How well is the child being reared by the former mate? Do the children have decent clothes? Are they getting attention? Are they getting a good education? Are they even being fed adequately? Are they being motivated? Are good ethics and ideals being instilled in them? Remember that, practically, possession is nine-tenths of the law; whoever has physical custody will likely to have the greatest influence on the children's lives and well-being.

Indeed, custody decisions aren't always fair to all parties, and the child may end up living with a parent who lacks the will or the means to do a decent job of child-rearing.

Further, the trauma of divorce for both the child and the parent, and the havoc it can bring, such as moving and dividing the family's possessions, add to the difficulty of creating a stable world for the children.

And as children get older, the absence of a strong father or mother may lead to behavioral and emotional problems. Adding new stepparents, and possibly new stepbrothers and stepsisters, as well as other new relatives, can further complicate the child's search for a normal family life.

Recognizing that millions of children survive these situations is no small measure of their durability. But we will never fully know the extent to which all of this affects child development. The evidence, discussed earlier, is not especially encouraging.

As for the noncustodial spouse, he or she may face other pressures. It is easy to feel left out, and absence may really make the heart grow fonder. Some parents, on the other hand, may actually welcome a child-free atmosphere; certainly there will be less daily stress, particularly in a new marriage, if the children are neither seen nor heard. But this could lead to feelings of guilt and inadequacy. Again, the stepparent may be blamed for the situation.

And some parents just shun responsibility. They probably did so during the marriage, and are more than happy to do so after the divorce. These people are unlikely to assume their fair share of the financial burdens as well. If you are divorcing someone who fits this description, don't anticipate great personality changes when the marriage is history. So get a good lawyer.

ALWAYS BE READY

Finally, the noncustodial parent must always be prepared to assume custody. The custodial parent may die, may abdicate responsibility, or may remarry and decide to streamline his or her life. Also, the child may decide that living with the other parent would be a better deal for any number of reasons.

Frequently, children switch between parents to play on their sympathy and guilt—an attempt, perhaps, to get a more accommodating living environment, or a greater degree of personal freedom. The geographic location of the parents may also play a role. One part of the country may be more attractive to the child as he or she grows up.

Certainly, the responsibilities of child-rearing can shift suddenly and without warning. Be prepared.

ABSENCE MAKES ME WORRY

Barbara Norwood was somewhat afraid when she agreed to let her ex-husband have custody of their two children, Amy, seven, and Alexander, nine. For a variety of practical reasons, though, she felt that this was best for both herself and her children. Little did she anticipate the implications of her decision.

For the first six months after the divorce, everything seemed to go pretty well. The children visited Barbara on weekends, and seemed happy and well-adjusted, aside from the obvious immediate impact of the divorce itself. But all in all, she felt that they were holding up pretty well and that they were getting a decent amount of attention from their father.

After another couple of months, however, the picture changed. When Amy and Alexander would visit their mother, she began to notice that they were poorly attended to; their clothes were falling apart, their physical appearance grew worse and worse, and they seemed to be less disciplined with every passing day.

A year after the divorce, Barbara finally realized that her former husband—who was never great for helping with the children and the house anyway—wasn't really doing a decent job of taking care of the kids. The children had only looked good in the early months because the clothes were new and the kids managed to maintain things.

Realizing the true situation, Barbara was deeply disturbed and felt that she couldn't let it continue. Fourteen months after the break up, she went back to court and reopened the divorce proceedings. She requested custody of the children, which the father initially fought but eventually agreed to.

Within three months of Barbara's assuming custody, as difficult as it was for her while she was working, the children completely turned around in their attitudes and general wellbeing. Their father continued to do as little as possible, but Barbara wasn't overly disturbed; she felt that she had at least saved the children from potential disaster.

With her house in order and her children better attended to, Barbara began to move on with her life, and even started dating again. With her life beginning anew, she hoped to find a different mate, one more willing to participate in childrearing and in sharing household duties, as well as being a good provider and an all-around great person.

Part Four

The Commitments and the Answers

8

The Ongoing Challenge

Marriage vows say that your commitments are to last forever. When it comes to children from previous marriages, these vows are truest. Marrying someone with children (or you bringing children into a marriage) means accepting that they are not just around during their early, formative years or even while they are growing up or are in college. They are a presence and concern in your life forever.

Children do not really leave home. Some move away and live their own lives while many these days still live at home when they're in their 20s; others move back after college, a failed marriage, an illness, or other personal problems.

The Challenge: You Never Get Out from Under the Stepchildren

Making It Work: Create and Maintain Space; Set Limits

Just when you thought it was safe to enjoy the marriage, one of the children may reappear at your doorstep. Natural parents aren't likely to turn their own children away. You may end up with a grown person living with you for an indeterminate time. What's more, he or she may bring home a package:

his or her own children, girlfriends, boyfriends, a spouse, or who knows what other friend or relative. Think about the marital stress that can endure as you deal with these possibilities.

In more extreme, but not uncommon, cases, the offspring may bring a variety of financial, social, emotional, drug, health, and other problems along to throw in your and your spouse's laps.

SO FAR YET SO NEAR

When the young adult is out of the house and living on his or her own, other problems can impinge on your marriage. Frequent requests for financial assistance are not exactly unheard of. We all like to help our children, but in remarriages there are other people and other needs to think about, too. And the former spouse may duck out of any responsibility.

The Challenge: The Stepchildren May Be a Constant Source of Demands and Impositions

Making It Work: Draw the Line and Make Clear What You Can and Cannot Do

Just when you are trying to rear your own children, the stepchildren may be making yet more financial and emotional demands. Children often share problems with their parents, so telephone calls concerning marital, girlfriend, boyfriend, and financial problems, accidents, run-ins with the law, medical problems, and difficulties with their own children can take some of the starch out of your own marriage.

There is no end to what can be thrown your way. The natural parent will probably be stressed out from worrying about his or her own children, and rightly so. But the stepparent may also be stressed, worrying about what crises will come up next. Even into middle age and later, a stepchild can disrupt his or her parent's new marriage. Some people never grow up, requiring constant help and draining the parents' emotional reservoirs.

You may even be confronted with the problems of your stepchild's children. Again, a whole range of problems, pressures, and difficulties can be thrust upon you. Do you really want to worry about your spouse's children, grandchildren, and perhaps even great-grandchildren for the next twenty or thirty years? Can you tolerate having all of these people at your financial and emotional trough?

THE MOVE-IN

John Reynolds was greatly saddened by the death of his wife, Mary. They had been together for twenty-one years. But with the strength he derived from his two children, he was able to get his feet back on the ground relatively soon after Mary's death. In fact, about eight months later, he became increasingly friendly with Elizabeth Thompson, an extremely pleasant woman whom he and his wife had known casually for several years.

Elizabeth's husband had also passed away after a long bout with cancer. She was left with two sons, both grown and living in another town not too far away.

John and Elizabeth's relationship grew, and within another seven months they got engaged. And since their children were on their own, they really never gave a second thought to the implications of children from prior marriages. In fact, both were astute enough to write wills leaving their assets to their own children. They recognized that, individually, they each had more than enough income and assets to live on and would probably leave an estate that neither one really needed.

All of the children attended the ceremony and everybody was happy that these two wonderful people would live and enjoy life together. None of the children, fortunately, resented the marriage, and all looked forward to a better life for this pair.

And things indeed went very well. Both John and Elizabeth were certain that they had made a good decision; they were well suited for each other and happy together.

One day, however, Elizabeth's older son, Tom, called and everything changed. He had lost his job and had run out of money. He was also leaving his wife. Could he move in with his mother and her new husband? he asked. Not wanting to abandon her own child, and after quickly consulting John and assuring him that this was a short-term arrangement, she consented. Within a week Tom moved in.

John immediately realized that he had made a mistake by letting his stepson move in. Although Tom was not a particularly disagreeable person, he wasn't overly friendly or helpful around the house, either. He was prone to coming in and out late and rather noisily; he made no contribution to the family household in terms of food, or cleaning up, or anything else. And even though he was 26, he expected his mother to do his laundry and, all in all, to take care of him. He expected John to do likewise.

The whole arrangement quickly grew tiring, especially for John. But Elizabeth was not surprised; she already knew what Tom's personality and habits were like.

Finally, John issued an ultimatum to Elizabeth: either he or Tom was moving out. She felt torn between her own child and her new husband and didn't really know what to do. Tom *offered no help or consolation to either parent and merely stated that he was having a tough time and would like their help.*

After a lot of discussion and some aggravation, John and Elizabeth eventually agreed that they would have Tom move into an apartment of his own, and they would also give him $600 a month until he got his life back together.

Tom reluctantly accepted this plan. Clearly, he wasn't eager to move and look after himself, even with financial support. Nor did he appreciate that $600 a month was a big chunk of money for his mother and stepfather. He did agree to seek employment more aggressively and to try to pare down his spending to match his income. He also said that he would try to be on his own within six months.

Fortunately, Tom got a job. Although it took him two months to leave his mother's house, he eventually did and began supporting himself. He even met a new, and serious, girlfriend. John and Elizabeth began to readjust to the life that they had originally wanted to pursue and hoped that all of their children would be able to take care of themselves.

What Is the Long-Term Commitment?

To reiterate, children are and should be a lifetime commitment for their natural parents. This commitment, however, is shirked by many parents, particularly after divorce.

This can take the form of alienation from the children, failure of former spouses to communicate, and other factors contributing to abandonment. Failure to assume financial and other parenting responsibilities is, unfortunately, all too commonplace in our nation these days.

As a stepparent, you may be thrust into a permanent parenting role that you do not enjoy. Then again, a harmonious, long-lasting, and rewarding attachment between you and your stepchildren may evolve. But often this isn't the reality. No one should become a stepparent assuming that once the children are grown, the responsibilities will be over. You have to assume a long-term perspective, realizing that your life will be changed forever. For better or worse, these are the facts that stepparents face.

> *The Challenge:* Grown Children Can Feel Alienated by a Parent's New Marriage
>
> *Making It Work:* Reinforce Your Love and Commitment to Them

OLDER DOESN'T MEAN BETTER

You might think that after the kids are grown and "gone," it doesn't really matter if the natural parents divorce. Some couples wait until the children are grown to go ahead with a long-desired divorce. And sometimes the absence of the children leaves the marriage without any common ground.

Surprisingly, grown children often resent their parents' divorcing later in their lives. Even when the kids are middle-aged and the parents are well along in years, this resentment may be strongly felt. They may feel that the divorce has destroyed their heritage. Their idealized picture of the family is shattered. They wonder how long their parents were unhappy, even though they may have had some inkling all along which they tried to ignore or discount. And they may blame themselves, just as younger children do.

When older parents remarry after divorce, or after the death of one of the natural parents, the "children" may still harbor great resentment against the new spouse. The stepparent may be viewed as stealing the parent and even as breaking up the family. If one of the parents has died, the stepparent may never equal the wonderful, but now deceased, parent. And sometimes children worry about the new spouse's hidden financial motives if the surviving spouse has significant assets.

The Challenge: Handling Hostilities
Making It Work: Be Realistic and Understanding, and Maintain Open Lines of Communication

Grown stepchildren may be angry with or reject the natural parent or the stepparent. It's not likely that they will accept the stepparent as a "real" parent, but rather view him or her as Mom's or Dad's new mate. You must consider these feelings and match your own expectations to reality.

Sometimes however, especially when a parent has died, the children may welcome the new spouse. A lot will depend on the extent to which the new spouse is seen as taking care of, and caring for, the natural parent. And a lot will depend on the natural parents' relationships in the past, the reasons for the divorce or death, and a whole host of other complex factors. A psychologist or psychiatrist may be useful in helping you understand the family dynamics that you face.

The Challenge Continues

To repeat, a stepparent's relationship with stepchildren does not end, at least as long as the marriage stays intact. And it is not even unheard of for a stepparent to divorce the stepchildren's natural parent, but continue to maintain warm relations with the children. More often, though, divorce ends relations with stepchildren.

When the stepchildren mature, they will likely marry and have children of their own. As a stepparent you then face the prospect of being a "stepgrandparent." This presents an opportunity to play yet another role in the marriage. Grandchildren usually give their grandparents incredible joy and pleasure, but not all stepparents will feel so elated by their stepchildren's kids.

Sometimes grandparents find themselves custodians of their own grandchildren. This happens most frequently when the parent dies or is incapacitated or when a parent gets involved with drugs or crime and can no longer function as a parent. The grandparents may feel obligated to step in and take over.

LIFE'S UNCERTAINTIES

Life is a challenge, and predicting the course of events is, of course, impossible. Many scenarios loom which could make life unpleasant or difficult for a stepparent. The stepchildren could become involved with crime, drugs, or other social problems. Like anyone else, they can lose their jobs, have their finances in disarray, have numerous psychological problems, get into accidents, get divorced, have children out of wedlock, and get into fights. Naturally, their problems are usually stressful for their parents.

The possibility of serious illness or injury always exists. As people age, the chances of some sort of disabling illness increases greatly. Accidents from work, automobiles, or motorcycles are a constant threat.

Should such a tragedy occur, the stepparent might have to help the natural parent care for the child, or even substitute for both natural parents if they are dead or incapacitated.

The stepchild might even have to move back into the parents' home.

Stepchildren may ask for financial help to set up a business, buy a house, or to meet other needs. They may ask the stepparent to co-sign for loans or pay off debts. All in all, these requests may call for a balancing act between the needs of new children and those of the stepchildren. The natural parent may want to do more for his or her children than the stepparent wants, a sure cause of marital stress. The other natural parent may be unwilling to do anything, leaving everything in the lap—and the bank account—of the stepparent and his or her spouse. The needs of two sets of children, the effort to keep the marriage intact, the spouses' preferences, and the stepparents' priorities may not all be compatible.

These scenarios may not be common, but they are worth thinking about. This is not to say that you shouldn't be there in times of need, *but do think about your priorities, and your own needs.*

9

Where Do We Go From Here?

By now it should be clear that the complexities of remarriage with children are profound. The social fabric of our nation has been rewoven. More than one million divorces and more than one million marriages occur each year in the United States. Half of all divorces involve children. *The numbers are staggering.*

The collective mental health and emotional stability of millions of children are a serious national concern. For everyone, the facts of life are far removed from the white-washed images that once flickered across old television screens.

The Challenge: Becoming Part of, or Staying in, a Stepfamily

Making It Work: Look Before You Leap; Work at It Every Day

If you are thinking about marrying someone who has children, the message is clear: be informed and understand what you may encounter. If you are already involved, this book can serve as an on-going guide, helping you to confront the forces you are already facing, and to plan.

And if you picked up this book because you have friends or family in these marriages, or are simply interested in the changing nature of our society, you should be able to see through the superficial picture of family life and into the intricate psychological, emotional, and financial world in which your friends and relatives live. Every family is different, but the concerns and issues that stepfamilies must deal with form a common bond.

There is no going back. We may rediscover fundamental truths and strengthen our emotional ties with each other in the future. We may strengthen the social structure of the family, and we may, as a society, move toward a more caring existence.

But things probably won't change appreciably in the foreseeable future. As never before, divorce is accepted by our society and will continue to be so. Men and women are no longer willing to tolerate unhappy or abusive relationships, or fundamentally unsatisfying lives.

The divorce rate may even increase. Fundamental changes in our legal and economic systems now make divorce easier and allow women, in particular, to earn a living on their own.

We can hope that we will rekindle our commitment to our children. Those marriages that can be saved, particularly when children are involved, will hopefully endure. But ultimately, our society, and we as individuals, *must accept and accommodate the realities of divorce and marriage.*

A Fundamentally Difficult Situation

Remarriage with children is a fundamentally unnatural situation. *Everyone* involved must make it work. Like living with a roommate, great accommodations are needed. When it works, it can be great, but when it fails it is a tremendously difficult and unpleasant arrangement. Almost like having lucky stars line up perfectly, everyone—natural parents, relatives, new spouses, and all the children—must also be in perfect alignment.

A LOOK AT YOUR OPTIONS

If you're not currently involved in a stepfamily, it's worth thinking about each of the alternatives and which may be the best avenue for you to pursue. None of these choices is necessarily ideal, but in truth there probably is no ideal or easy solution.

The Challenge: Taking an Alternative Path
Making It Work: Consider Alternatives to Marriage

One possibility, and a common one, is simply to live together rather than to marry. Many people live together so that they can maintain separate finances. For those who do not want more children, and for whom the institution of marriage itself is not all that "key" in their lives, living together can offer a very viable choice.

Many of the difficulties that come with stepchildren are less likely to seriously disrupt your life when you are not married. Finances can be kept separate so that money and the former spouse's contributions to child support need not be a critical issue. A lot of the emotional and social burdens can be avoided by living together.

Just the same, living together still means living with someone else's children with all that goes with it. It may also have a variety of adverse, longer-term, legal and financial consequences. And of course the absence of a marriage certificate may represent far less commitment between partners. And without that sense of commitment, having someone else's children around can be too much to bear.

For couples with teenagers, living together may be a workable consideration when you expect to marry later on when the children are out of the household. And since there is indeed no ideal solution, living together may offer, for the right pair, the best of both worlds.

Another choice that may appeal to some is simply not to divorce in the first place. Perhaps we should change our system, making it much harder to get married and much easier to get divorced. Theoretically, those people who *did* end up marrying would have a much greater chance of staying married, and, in the long run, the divorce rate would drop appreciably.

By not divorcing, one can obviously avoid the problems of stepfamilies. This should be taken seriously. A lot of people tend to give up on marriage without giving *to* marriage—making an all-out effort to help it succeed. When children are involved, it's especially worth going the extra mile to try to work things out. And the prevalence of sexually-transmitted diseases as well as economic and social problems are legitimate reasons for giving marriage a second chance.

Another consideration is neither to remarry nor to live with someone after divorce. This allows you full flexibility in rearing your own children the way you want without interference from any other partner.

This approach does not rule out living a full life, but it *does* define certain limits on future romance. At the least, it can be an excellent first step after divorce while you're getting your feet on the ground and figuring out what to do next.

Another possibility is to make sure that you don't get custody of the children. The noncustodial parent has the greatest freedom and flexibility to go on with life because he or she is not encumbered by the day-to-day burdens of child-rearing. Remarriage without children in tow will definitely be easier. The drawback, however, is that you may not get to see your children grow up and could suffer emotionally from the separation.

> *The Challenge:* You May Not Know How You Will React to the Situation
> *Making It Work:* Jump in Slowly

You can compromise—test the waters. You and your potential spouse can keep separate homes and spend time getting to know each other—and the children—better. Without taking the actual plunge, you can see how stepfamily life *might* go for you. Unfortunately, because of the lack of commitment and permanence in this experiment, your expectations may not be totally realistic. As anybody who has been through a marriage can attest, being romantically involved and being formally joined are two entirely different sets of circumstances. In no way can any arrangement short of marriage fully prepare the future stepparent for what really lies ahead. But at least each potential partner will be able to glean *some* idea of what lies down the road.

IF YOU GO AHEAD

Once the marriage contract is signed, a whole additional set of considerations and alternatives awaits. Marriage from a legal, and certainly from a moral, perspective is a significant, concrete commitment. And when the honeymoon is over, it is much more difficult to make changes in the situation.

So what happens if things don't quite work out as well as

you had hoped? What if the *worst* possibilities turn into realities? If they do, there is help available, and there are alternatives to pursue.

As in all families, getting along in stepfamilies is a matter of *compromise and commitment.* The inherent complexity and conflicts of the situation simply mean that there is no easy, ideal answer. Finding accommodations, being flexible, and having everybody agree on ways of solving problems are the only alternatives. The search for accommodation can be helped along in a number of ways.

Psychologists who specialize in counseling stepfamilies recommend a number of approaches to make discussions and the search for compromises easier. One frequently suggested idea is to hold regular family meetings to discuss any problems and to come up with possible solutions. Unfortunately, children and adults are not always totally rational. Almost like the peace-seeking efforts in the Middle East, family discussions may lead to the resolution of minor problems and the exacerbation of major ones.

A less democratic way is for the natural parents and stepparents to simply lay down the law and explain that "this is the way things will be, and we will follow these rules." Still, every intelligent parent knows that even with strong, positive reinforcement for the children, carrying out these mandates is not easy. But, as in the rest of the world, discussion and compromise are certainly preferable to warfare.

Another possible answer is to send the children (or some of them) to live with the other parent. As painful as this may be for everybody involved, if this is what it takes to save a troubled marriage, this may be the answer. The noncustodial parent will obviously have a much easier time in living life and in trying to maintain a new marriage than will the custodial parent. This might even be a viable approach on a short-term, rather than permanent, basis to allow the normal difficulties of the marriage to work out.

Psychologists warn against doing anything that implies that children are the cause of either the divorce or of any marital stress. While this is desirable, it may not be completely doable; children are naturally egocentric and will be in the thick of things. Moreover, most marital difficulties are pretty obvious to them—particularly if they have already been through one divorce.

For those trying to hold the family together and cope with stepchildren, there are a number of ways to get help. Relatives and friends can be especially valuable in providing general emotional support for all members of the family. Indeed, having close family and friends often helps one cope with all of life's trials. A former spouse who is supportive and helpful, although probably rare, is also of immense value to the custodial parents.

Professional counseling is another way for blended families to get help in working out problems. Psychologists, licensed clinical social workers who specialize in family and marriage counseling, psychiatrists, and even your family physician may be a source of help. Problems that are a result of unacceptable behavior among stepchildren might be evaluated by pediatricians or by child and adolescent psychiatrists and psychologists. In seeking such assistance, be sure to look toward those professionals with concrete experience in dealing with stepfamilies. An outside perspective may be useful if you, your spouse, or the stepchildren are too immersed in the emotional side of things to be objective or to negotiate with each other. Professional insights into the "tricks of the trade" that seem to work in these complex and unique family environments may work for you.

It may help to know that you are not alone. There is a national association dedicated to stepparents. The Stepfamily Association of America, Inc., provides publications and other educational assistance and supports the formation of local chapters. Information is available by writing to the Association at 215 Centennial Mall S., Suite 212, Lincoln, NE 68508, or by telephoning (402) 477-STEP.

Local stepfamily associations now exist throughout the country, and new ones are always being formed. The national association also provides assistance and information to anyone interested in forming a local chapter. The local chapters focus on forming support groups for such families. The mere existence of the organization says a lot about the need for help.

A Few Other Thoughts on Being a Stepparent

A fundamental flaw in many marriages, especially remarriages, is the failure of both spouses to recognize and acknowledge the existence of a problem. Problems can fester, and when they involve such basic issues as how to deal with children, their magnitude can grow and eventually threaten the marriage itself. And silence is not a solution.

Since the stepchildren are often the focus, for better or worse, of many of the frictions of stepfamilies, it is especially important that both spouses agree to certain fundamentals at the start. These include their roles in rearing and disciplining the children.

Discipline is a particularly thorny issue. It's difficult in the best of circumstances, and especially so for older children.

Very frequently, stepchildren do not see the stepparent as an authority figure. If the natural parent, and preferably both natural parents, does not let the children know that the stepparent *does* have authority, much will be lost in trying to make the stepfamily work.

Many stepparents probably feel that there should be a Stepparents' Bill of Rights—that everything should be clearly spelled out for them. But even if there was such an official document, it wouldn't mean much; your rights are what you carve out for yourself.

Remember that stepparents are due their dignity, privacy, respect, and privileges. If your rights are violated, you either have to accept it or fight it. This can be a very tough battle and one with many casualties. Decide what is worth the struggle. Set your own priorities and stand up for them, know what is most valuable to you, and realize what makes life enjoyable.

When your spouse clearly agrees that the marriage is of paramount importance and that you as a stepparent have the same basic rights as anyone else, the situation can work. Otherwise, it may be a lonely road, but it is one that your life and happiness depend upon.

Then there is the matter of expectations. *It is crucial for everyone involved to understand the difficulties of stepfamilies and to be realistic about lifestyle, discipline, finances, and many other matters.* Unrealistic visions, such as seeing family life as one big holiday without any problems, can set everyone up for a fall. The facts are that this is a difficult situation to be in, and that everyone has to make the best of it by trying to accommodate other's needs and concerns. Knowing this is the first step helps in avoiding disappointments and disasters.

Depending on the age of the children, it can be fruitful to sit down with them at the start and explain the nature of stepfamilies and what to expect and what not to expect. An honest appraisal of what life may be like will help the children face the future.

Similarly, the husband and wife may need to have a reality check. Identify areas where problems could develop and you may help avert them.

In some situations, it may be best for the stepparent to adopt the stepchildren. Adoption may enhance the bonds between the stepparent and the stepchildren and is well worth exploring when the other natural parent is deceased. As always, though, get legal advice before you leap.

CONTEMPLATING MARRIAGE

So what can you do if you are contemplating a marriage that involves children, either from your or your spouse's prior marriage? Is it too unromantic and calculating to marry with your eyes open?

These are not easy questions. Reason does tend to dampen romance. But you must try your best to answer them. You owe it to yourself, to your future spouse, and to the children, present and future.

Despite societal taboos, there is nothing bad or selfish in talking about all of this with your future mate. Open communication is one of the best ways to a good, strong marriage. But if one—or both—person is unwilling, or unable, to discuss the children's involvement in the marriage, then the course ahead may be perilous.

So before getting married, consider these early warning signs that often suggest trouble down the road:

- Children who have behavioral, social, or emotional problems

- Children with physical problems
- Natural parents who do not communicate
- Children who are hostile towards a future stepparent
- A natural parent who expects the stepparent-to-be to solve financial problems
- A natural parent who hopes to create a "traditional" family life for his or her children through remarriage
- Emotional, psychological, or other problems with the spouse-to-be
- A lack of *total* commitment by the natural parent to the new spouse and to the marriage
- A lack of reality in everyone's perspective

If any red flags appear, reconsider. Carefully analyze the financial, emotional, and social aspects of your marriage.

Lay it all out. Express your concerns and apprehensions. Try to come up with solutions and compromises that both of you can live with for a very long time. Keep in mind that every aspect of your life will be affected and forever changed!

Be Realistic

If the children are young when a parent remarries, and especially if one of the natural parents is dead, bonding and relationships between them and their stepparents will likely be easier and more fulfilling. By the same token older children tend to be less receptive to a "new" parent, and less likely to work at a more traditional relationship. Teenagers can be especially difficult and even adult children can be hostile and unreceptive!

Indeed, children of any age may be profoundly affected by divorce and the more harmful the effects, the more likely it is that his or her relationship with the stepparent will be strained.

Stepparents may have to live full- or part-time with children who at best view them as friends and at worst as enemies.

This antagonism may reflect underlying problems for which the stepparent becomes a convenient scapegoat. Growing up means facing obstacles and everyone needs ways to vent anger or discontent. Unfortunately, children may see stepparents as natural lightning rods.

Each Child Is Different

If there is more than one stepchild, they may "gang up" on the stepparent. The stepparent may even have different feelings for each of the children, and interactions can vary tremendously from child to child.

Try to develop positive relationships with each of the children independently. Naturally, it may not be possible to cultivate warm relationships with *all* of the stepchildren. You will be rewarded by those with whom you can build a rapport. And sometimes a divide-and-conquer strategy can defuse any group animosity.

Also, play down hostilities and don't criticize the stepchildren. This may be quite difficult to do when dealing with the practical, day-to-day side of life, however. Think about how much self-control you have.

WHEN IT DOESN'T WORK

If the chemistry just doesn't work, it may be necessary for people to go their separate ways. This can be done without divorce. The stepparent should focus on the marriage and on any new children. The stepchildren can focus on their own lives with some reasonable accommodation among all parties.

As the children get older, if they are responsible, an accommodation may be workable. Both natural parents will have to be highly responsible for this to work.

Survival hints for stepparents include:

- Making the marriage first in your priorities
- Openly communicating with your spouse
- Having realistic expectations
- Understanding the limits of affection
- Putting things in perspective and not taking them too personally
- Knowing that there are no guarantees
- Keeping a sense of humor
- Focusing on the positive aspects of the marriage

AND WHEN IT WORKS

Being a stepparent can be extremely rewarding. The opportunity to guide youngsters can be as fulfilling to a stepparent as it is to a natural parent. When the other natural parent is out of the picture, and when the children are young, the stepparent can assume a more motherly or fatherly role. And even for older couples who have grown children, being the family newcomer can be a warm and welcoming experience. All it takes is good rapport and strong emotional support on all sides.

Even so, keep in mind that children develop differently and sometimes unpredictably. Many factors may be beyond the control of either the natural parent or the stepparent. Matters such as the genetic makeup, which affects intelligence and personality, is beyond the control of anyone.

As noted earlier, making accurate predictions is impossible.

How children will develop, what kind of relationships they will have with their natural parents or stepparents, and the impact of divorce on their development are all largely unknowns. And for younger children, there is less basis for prediction.

Are you the right person for this lifestyle? Many people are not. An *ideal stepparent profile* might include the following qualities:

- A sense of flexibility
- An easygoing attitude toward children and their behaviors
- A healthy view of money
- A belief that the other partner can make good key decisions
- A trust that the natural parent is totally committed to the marriage
- A knowledge that the natural parent can work with the needs of the children and the spouse

Indeed, remarriage with children is a gamble. The consequences take years to unfold, and by the time they do, it may be too late to handle them simply. It's best to step back from time to time and see what is happening along the way.

What the Stepparent Risks

A stepparent may be risking more than he or she realizes. Physical health can easily be tested by stress from the children and spouse. Financially supporting everyone through hard times as well as the physical labor of child rearing can take their toll.

Likewise, the emotional and psychological demands can be equally great. Little pressures every day can build up. The strength of your marriage may be constantly tested. The many potentially unpleasant aspects of the situation, such as dealing with the ex-spouse, can make everything even worse. Your very sanity can be pushed to its limits.

Then there are the financial risks. The stepparent may lose most that he or she has accumulated and may also sacrifice future savings. And after all of the costs, the emotional payback may be minimal or nonexistent.

If things are beyond repair, there may be no safety valves or easy outs, especially if you have new children. But then again, everything may indeed work out fine.

KEY POINTS FOR SUCCESS

To pull things together, here are the eleven key points for successful stepparenting:

1. Make the marriage the number-one consideration.
2. Keep your eyes open.
3. Anticipate and plan for the future.
4. Recognize and deal with the relationships between the parents and children.
5. Understand the realities.
6. Work on maximizing the marriage's underlying potential.
7. Know the financial, psychological, social, and emotional implications of the situation and deal with each.
8. Open and maintain good lines of communication among the key parties.
9. Accept the relationships for what they are.
10. At the start, be open about all of the complexities and stresses that may exist.
11. Always count your blessings.

Keeping your eyes on the "big picture" is the best way to follow the path. Deal with the day-to-day nitty-gritty, but always remember your long-term objectives. Focus on the positives. Know what you and your spouse want from the relationship.

As in *any* family, success is measured in growth and individual happiness. Failure is measured in dissension and dissatisfaction, and possibly, in divorce. But don't give in to discouragement. It can work, but *you* have to make it work.

ADDITIONAL SOURCES OF INFORMATION

Stepfamily Association of America, Inc.
215 Centennial Mall S., Suite 212
Lincoln, NE 68508

Telephone: (402) 477-STEP
(800) 735-0329

Available resources include:
  -publications for adults and children
  -referrals to local support groups/chapters
  -chapter development materials
  -periodic magazine
  -annual membership

GENERAL INTEREST BOOKS

Hal W. Anderson and Gail S. Anderson: *Mom and Dad are Divorced, But I'm Not: Parenting After Divorce.* Chicago, Nelson-Hall, 1981.
William Beer: *American Stepfamilies.* New Brunswick, NJ, Transaction Publishers, 1992.
Joel Block: *To Marry Again.* New York, Grosset & Dunlap, 1979.
Fredrick Capaldi and Barbara McRae: *Stepfamilies: A Cooperative Responsibility.* New York, Vision Books, 1979.
Lynne McNamara: *Separation, Divorce, and After.* New York, University of Queensland Press, 1982.

Frank Zagone: *How to Adopt Your Stepchildren in California.* Berkeley, CA, Nolo Press, 1979. *Note: Laws vary by state.*

Donna Smith: *Stepmothering.* New York, Harvester Wheatsheaf, 1990.

Ester Wald: *The Remarried Family: Challenge and Promise.* New York, York Family Service Association of America, 1981.

ACADEMIC BOOKS

William Beer, Editor: *Relative Strangers: Studies of Stepfamily Processes.* Totowa, NJ, Rowman and Littlefield, 1988.

Ellen J. Gruber: *Stepfamilies: A Guide to the Sources and Resources.* New York, Garland, 1986.

Kay Pasley and Marilyn Ihinger-Tallman: *Remarriage and Stepparenting: Current Research and Theory.* New York, Gilford Press, 1987.

Judith DeB. Sadler: *Families in Transition: An Annotated Bibliography.* Hamden, CT, Archon Books, 1988.

Emily Visher and John Visher: *Stepfamilies: A Guide to Working With Stepparents and Stepchildren.* New York, Brunner/Mazel, 1979.

UNITED STATES GOVERNMENT PUBLICATIONS

Bureau of the Census: *Stepchildren and Their Families.* Washington, D.C., U.S. Government Printing Office, Statistical Brief, SB-1-89, 1989.

Sharyn R. Duffin: *Yours, Mine, and Ours: Tips for Stepparents.* Washington, D.C., U.S. Department of Health, Education, and Welfare, publication number (ADM) 78-676, 1978.

Renato Espinoza and Yvonne Newman: *Stepparenting, with Annotated Bibliography.* Washington, D.C., U.S. Department of Health, Education, and Welfare, Public Health Service, publication number (ADM) 78-579, 1979.

SELECTED TECHNICAL SOURCES

Block, J.H., Block, J., Gjerde, P.F. "Parental Functioning and the Home Environment in Families of Divorce: Prospective and Concurrent Analyses." *Child Dev* 57(4):827–40. 1986.

Bumpass, L., "Children and Marital Disruption: A Replication and Update." *Demography* 21(1):71–82. 1984.

Dawson, D.A. "Family structure and children's health: United States, 1988." National Center for Health Statistics. Vital Health Stat 10(178). 1991.

Emery, R.E. "Interpersonal Conflict and the Children of Discord and Divorce." *Psychol Bulletin* 92:310–30. 1982.

Guidabaldi, J., Perry, J.D., Cleminshaw, H.K. "The Legacy of Parental Divorce: A Nationwide Study of Family Status and Selected Mediating Variables on Children's Academic and Social Competencies." In: Lakey, B.B., Kazdin, A.E., eds. *Advances in Child Clinical Psychology*, vol 7. New York: Plenum. 1984.

Hess, R.D., Camara, K.A. "Post-divorce Family Relationships as Mediating Factors in the Consequences of Divorce for Children." *J Social Issues* 35(1):79–96. 1979.

Kellam, S.G., Ensminger, M.E., Turner, R.J. "Family Structure and the Mental Health of Children." *Arch Gen Psychiatry* 34(11):1012–22. 1977.

National Center for Health Statistics, K.A. London, 1989. *Children of Divorce. Vital and Health Statistics. Series 21, No. 46.* DHHS Pub. No. (PHS) 89-1924. Public Health Service. Washington: U.S. Government Printing Office.

National Center for Health Statistics. Births, marriages, divorces, and deaths for 1991. Monthly vital statistics report; vol 40 no 12. Hyattsville, Maryland: Public Health Service. 1992.

Porter, B., O'Leary, K.D. "Types of Marital Discord and Child Behavior Problems." *J Abnorm Child Psychol* 8:287–95. 1980.

Thornton, A., Freedman, D. 1983. "The Changing American Family. *Population Bulletin.* 38(4):1–44.

ADDITIONAL SOURCES OF INFORMATION

Weitzman, L. J. 1985. "The Divorce Revolution: The Unexpected Social and Economic Consequences for Women and Children in America." New York: The Free Press.

Zill, N. "Behavior, Achievement, and Health Problems among Children in Stepfamilies: Findings from a National Survey of Child Health. In: Hethrington, E.M., Arasteh, J.D., eds. *Impact of Divorce, Single Parenting, and Stepparenting on Children.* Hillsdale, NJ: Lawrence Erlbaum Associates. 1988.

ABOUT THE AUTHOR

Stephen J. Williams is a professor and head of the Division of Health Services Administration at San Diego State University's Graduate School of Public Health.

Widely published, Dr. Williams is the author of thirteen books and nearly one hundred articles on education, health, and human services. His books have sold more than one hundred thousand copies and his textbooks are considered among the best in their fields.

Dr. Williams also directs a $2 million study for the U.S. government on preventive health services under Medicare. He has previously served on the faculty of the University of Washington and is a graduate of Carnegie-Mellon University, the Massachusetts Institute of Technology, and Harvard University.

Dr. Williams is the stepfather of two sons.

Additional copies of *The Stepparent Challenge: A Primer for Making It Work* may be ordered by sending a check for $13.95 plus postage and handling (please add $2.00 for the first copy, $1.00 for each additional copy) to:

MasterMedia Limited
17 East 89th Street
New York, NY 10128
(212) 260-5600
(800) 334-8232
(212) 546-7638 (fax)

Dr. Williams is available for speeches and seminars. Please contact MasterMedia's Speakers' Bureau for availability and fee arrangement by calling Tony Colao at (908) 359-1612.

OTHER MASTERMEDIA BOOKS

To order MasterMedia books, either visit your local bookstore or call (800) 334-8232.

THE PREGNANCY AND MOTHERHOOD DIARY: Planning the First Year of Your Second Career, by Susan Schiffer Stautberg, is the first and only undated appointment diary that shows how to manage pregnancy and career. ($12.95 spiral-bound)

CITIES OF OPPORTUNITY: Finding the Best Place to Work, Live and Prosper in the 1990's and Beyond, by Dr. John Tepper Marlin, explores the job and living options for the next decade and into the next century. This consumer guide and handbook, written by one of the world's experts on cities, selects and features forty-six American cities and metropolitan areas. ($13.95 paper, $24.95 cloth)

THE DOLLARS AND SENSE OF DIVORCE, by Dr. Judith Briles, is the first book to combine practical tips on overcoming the legal hurdles by planning finances before, during, and after divorce. ($10.95 paper)

OUT THE ORGANIZATION: New Career Opportunities for the 1990s, by Robert and Madeleine Swain, is written for the millions of Americans whose jobs are no longer safe, whose companies are not loyal, and who face futures of uncertainty. It gives advice on finding a new job or starting your own business. ($12.95 paper)

AGING PARENTS AND YOU: A Complete Handbook to Help You Help Your Elders Maintain a Healthy, Productive and Independent Life, by Eugenia Anderson-Ellis, is a complete guide to providing care to aging relatives. It gives practical advice and resources to the adults who are helping their elders lead productive and independent lives. Revised and updated. ($9.95 paper)

CRITICISM IN YOUR LIFE: How to Give It, How to Take It, How to Make It Work for You, by Dr. Deborah Bright, offers practical advice, in an upbeat, readable, and realistic fashion, for turning criticism into control. Charts and diagrams guide the reader into managing criticism from bosses, spouses, children, friends, neighbors, in-laws, and business relations. ($17.95 cloth)

BEYOND SUCCESS: How Volunteer Service Can Help You Begin Making a Life Instead of Just a Living, by John F. Raynolds III and Eleanor Raynolds, C.B.E., is a unique how-to book targeted at business and professional people considering volunteer work, senior citizens who wish to fill leisure time meaningfully, and students trying out various career options. The book is filled with interviews with celebrities, CEOs, and average citizens who talk about the benefits of service work. ($19.95 cloth)

MANAGING IT ALL: Time-Saving Ideas for Career, Family, Relationships, and Self, by Beverly Benz Treuille and Susan Schiffer Stautberg, is written for women who are juggling careers and families. Over two hundred career women (ranging from a TV anchorwoman to an investment banker) were interviewed. The book contains many humorous anecdotes on saving time and improving the quality of life for self and family. ($9.95 paper)

YOUR HEALTHY BODY, YOUR HEALTHY LIFE: How to Take Control of Your Medical Destiny, by Donald B. Louria, M.D., provides precise advice and strategies that will help you to live a long and healthy life. Learn also about nutrition, exercise, vitamins, and medication, as well as how to control risk factors for major diseases. Revised and updated. ($12.95 paper)

THE CONFIDENCE FACTOR: How Self-Esteem Can Change Your Life, by Dr. Judith Briles, is based on a nationwide survey of six thousand men and women. Briles explores why women so often feel a lack of self-confidence and have a poor opinion of themselves. She offers step-by-step advice on becoming the person you want to be. ($9.95 paper, $18.95 cloth)

THE SOLUTION TO POLLUTION: 101 Things You Can Do to Clean Up Your Environment, by Laurence Sombke, offers step-by-step techniques on how to conserve more energy, start a recycling center, choose biodegradable products, and even proceed with individual environmental cleanup projects. ($7.95 paper)

TAKING CONTROL OF YOUR LIFE: The Secrets of Successful Enterprising Women, by Gail Blanke and Kathleen Walas, is based on the authors' professional experience with Avon Products' Women of Enterprise Awards, given each year to outstanding women entrepreneurs. The authors offer a specific plan to help you gain control over your life, and include business tips and quizzes as well as beauty and lifestyle information. ($17.95 cloth)

SIDE-BY-SIDE STRATEGIES: How Two-Career Couples Can Thrive in the Nineties, by Jane Hershey Cuozzo and S. Diane Graham, describes how two-career couples can learn the difference between competing with a spouse and becoming a supportive power partner. Published in hardcover as *Power Partners.* ($10.95 paper, $19.95 cloth)

DARE TO CONFRONT! How to Intervene When Someone You Care About Has an Alcohol or Drug Problem, by Bob Wright and Deborah George Wright, shows the reader how to use the step-by-step methods of professional interventionists to motivate drug-dependent people to accept the help they need. ($17.95 cloth)

WORK WITH ME! How to Make the Most of Office Support Staff, by Betsy Lazary, shows you how to find, train, and nurture the "perfect" assistant and how to best utilize your support staff professionals. ($9.95 paper)

MANN FOR ALL SEASONS: Wit and Wisdom from The Washington Post's *Judy Mann,* by Judy Mann, shows the columnist at her best as she writes about women, families, and the impact and politics of the women's revolution. ($9.95 paper, $19.95 cloth)

OTHER MASTERMEDIA BOOKS

THE SOLUTION TO POLLUTION IN THE WORKPLACE, by Laurence Sombke, Terry M. Robertson and Elliot M. Kaplan, supplies employees with everything they need to know about cleaning up their workspace, including recycling, using energy efficiently, conserving water, and buying recycled products and nontoxic supplies. ($9.95 paper)

THE ENVIRONMENTAL GARDENER: The Solution to Pollution for Lawns and Gardens, by Laurence Sombke, focuses on what each of us can do to protect our endangered plant life. A practical sourcebook and shopping guide. ($8.95 paper)

THE LOYALTY FACTOR: Building Trust in Today's Workplace, by Carol Kinsey Goman, Ph.D., offers techniques for restoring commitment and loyalty in the workplace. ($9.95 paper)

DARE TO CHANGE YOUR JOB—AND YOUR LIFE, by Carole Kanchier, Ph.D., provides a look at career growth and development throughout the life cycle. ($9.95 paper)

MISS AMERICA: In Pursuit of the Crown, by Ann-Marie Bivans, is an authorized guidebook to the Pageant, containing eyewitness accounts, complete historical data, and a realistic look at the trials and triumphs of the potential Miss Americas. ($19.95 paper, $27.50 cloth)

POSITIVELY OUTRAGEOUS SERVICE: New and Easy Ways to Win Customers for Life, by T. Scott Gross, identifies what the consumers of the nineties really want and how businesses can develop effective marketing strategies to answer those needs. ($14.95 paper)

BREATHING SPACE: Living and Working at a Comfortable Pace in a Sped-Up Society, by Jeff Davidson, helps readers to handle information and activity overload, and gain greater control over their lives. ($10.95 paper)

TWENTYSOMETHING: Managing and Motivating Today's New Work Force, by Lawrence J. Bradford, Ph.D., and Claire Raines, M.A., examines the work orientation of the younger generation,

OTHER MASTERMEDIA BOOKS

offering managers in businesses of all kinds a practical guide to better understand and supervise their young employees. ($22.95 cloth)

REAL LIFE 101: The Graduate's Guide to Survival, by Susan Kleinman, supplies welcome advice to those facing "real life" for the first time, focusing on work, money, health, and how to deal with freedom and responsibility. ($9.95 paper)

BALANCING ACTS! Juggling Love, Work, Family, and Recreation, by Susan Schiffer Stautberg and Marcia L. Worthing, provides strategies to achieve a balanced life by reordering priorities and setting realistic goals. ($12.95 paper)

REAL BEAUTY . . . REAL WOMEN: A Handbook for Making the Best of Your Own Good Looks, by Kathleen Walas, International Beauty and Fashion Director of Avon Products, offers expert advice on beauty and fashion to women of all ages and ethnic backgrounds. ($19.50 paper)

THE LIVING HEART BRAND NAME SHOPPER'S GUIDE (Revised and Updated), by Michael E. DeBakey, M.D., Antonio M. Gotto, Jr., M.D., D. Phil., Lynne W. Scott, M.A., R.D./L.D., and John P. Foreyt, Ph.D., lists brand-name supermarket products that are low in fat, saturated fatty acids, and cholesterol. ($14.95 paper)

MANAGING YOUR CHILD'S DIABETES, by Robert Wood Johnson IV, Sale Johnson, Casey Johnson, and Susan Kleinman, brings help to families trying to understand diabetes and control its effects. ($10.95 paper)

STEP FORWARD: Sexual Harassment in the Workplace, What You Need to Know, by Susan L. Webb, presents the facts for dealing with sexual harassment on the job. ($9.95 paper)

A TEEN'S GUIDE TO BUSINESS: The Secrets to a Successful Enterprise, by Linda Menzies, Oren S. Jenkins, and Rickell R. Fisher, provides solid information about starting your own business or working for one. ($7.95 paper)

OTHER MASTERMEDIA BOOKS

GLORIOUS ROOTS: Recipes for Healthy, Tasty Vegetables, by Laurence Sombke, celebrates the taste, texture, and versatility of root vegetables. Contains recipes for appetizers, soups, stews, and baked, broiled, and stir-fried dishes—even desserts. ($12.95 paper)

THE OUTDOOR WOMAN: A Handbook to Adventure, by Patricia Hubbard and Stan Wass, details the lives of adventurous outdoor women and offers their ideas on how you can incorporate exciting outdoor experiences into your life. ($14.95 paper)

FLIGHT PLAN FOR LIVING: The Art of Self-Encouragement, by Patrick O'Dooley, is a life guide organized like a pilot's flight checklist, which ensures you'll be flying "clear on top" throughout your life. ($17.95 cloth)

HOW TO GET WHAT YOU WANT FROM ALMOST ANYBODY, by T. Scott Gross, shows how to get great service, negotiate better prices, and always get what you pay for. ($9.95 paper)

FINANCIAL SAVVY FOR WOMEN: A Money Book for Women of All Ages, by Dr. Judith Briles, divides a woman's monetary lifespan into six phases, discusses the specific areas to be addressed at each stage, and demonstrates how to create a sound lifelong money game plan. ($14.95 paper)

TEAMBUILT: Making Teamwork Work, by Mark Sanborn, teaches business how to improve productivity, without increasing resources or expenses, by building teamwork among employers. ($19.95 cloth)

THE BIG APPLE BUSINESS AND PLEASURE GUIDE: 501 Ways to Work Smarter, Play Harder, and Live Better in New York City, by Muriel Siebert and Susan Kleinman, offers visitors and New Yorkers alike advice on how to do business in the city as well as how to enjoy its attractions. ($9.95 paper)

MIND YOUR OWN BUSINESS: And Keep It in the Family, by Marcy Syms, COO of Syms Corporation, is an effective guide for any

OTHER MASTERMEDIA BOOKS

organization, small or large, facing what is documented to be the toughest step in managing a family business—making the transition to the new generation. ($18.95 cloth)

KIDS WHO MAKE A DIFFERENCE, by Joyce M. Roché and Marie Rodriguez, with Phyllis Schneider, is a surprising and inspiring document of some of today's toughest challenges being met—by teenagers and kids! Their courage and creativity allowed them to find practical solutions. ($8.95 paper; with photos)

ROSEY GRIER'S ALL-AMERICAN HEROES: Multicultural Success Stories, by Roosevelt "Rosey" Grier, is a wonderful collection of personal histories, told in their own words by prominent African-Americans, Latins, Asians, and native Americans; each tells of the people in their lives and choices they made in achieving public acclaim and personal success. ($9.95 paper; with photos)

OFFICE BIOLOGY: Why Tuesday Is the Most Productive Day and Other Relevant Facts for Survival in the Workplace, by Edith Weiner and Arnold Brown, teaches how in the '90s and beyond we will be expected to work smarter, take better control of our health, adapt to advancing technology, and improve our lives in ways that are not too costly or resource-intensive. ($21.95 cloth)

ON TARGET: Enhance Your Life and Ensure Your Success, by Jeri Sedlar and Rick Miners, is a neatly woven tapestry of insights on career and life issues gathered from audiences across the country. This feedback has been crystalized into a highly readable guidebook for exploring who you are and how to go about getting what you want from your career and your life. ($11.95 paper)